DANIEL IN THE CRITICS' DEN

Books by Josh McDowell:

Daniel in the Critics' Den
More Than a Carpenter
More Evidence That Demands a Verdict
Evidence That Demands a Verdict

Josh McDowell

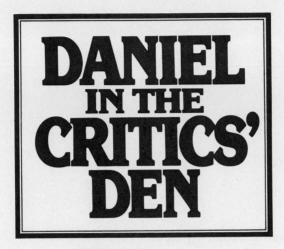

DANIEL IN THE CRITICS' DEN

**Historical Evidence
for the Authenticity of the
Book of Daniel**

CAMPUS CRUSADE FOR CHRIST INTERNATIONAL

Library of Congress Catalog Card Number: 78-71246
ISBN 0-918956-44-7   CCC 40-09-11

Library of Congress Cataloging in Publication Data

McDowell, Josh.
    Daniel in the critics' den.

    "A Campus Crusade for Christ book."
    Bibliography:
    1. Bible. O.T. Daniel — Criticism, interpretation, etc. I. Title.
BS1555.2.M32   224'.5'06   78-71246
ISBN 0-918956-44-7

This is an original Campus Crusade for Christ book, published by:
    Here's Life Publishers, Inc.
    A Ministry of Campus Crusade for Christ
    P.O. Box 1576
    San Bernardino, CA 92402

To two very close friends and associates

RON RALSTON and DON STEWART

with deep appreciation for their love,
friendship, constant encouragement and
help in writing this book.

Table of Contents

Preface
Why *Daniel in the Critics' Den?*

There are various reasons for adding this third volume to my first two books, *Evidence That Demands a Verdict* and *More Evidence That Demands a Verdict:*

(1) All the material could not be put into two volumes.

(2) I have received many requests from laymen, students, professors and pastors for material dealing with the Book of Daniel and its authenticity. University students are taking courses from professors steeped in one view; the student and layman who are studying Daniel, because of a lack of background, find themselves being brainwashed, not educated. They have no basis from which to answer and usually no sources to develop a positive response to what they are taught. Instead of responding with positive evidence, the student and layman are intimidated.

(3) There seems to be a need to counteract the "absoluteness" of so many university textbooks and seminary and Sunday school curriculum on Daniel.

DO WHAT WITH IT?

It is my desire that this book give Christian believers the confidence and knowledge to speak up. Christian students will be able to use this material to write papers, give speeches and interject their convictions about Jesus Christ and the Scriptures in the classroom. It should give laymen and pastors greater credibility in teaching.

THE TERM "RADICAL CRITIC"

The terms "radical critic" and "radical criticism" have been chosen as convenient ones to indicate those who basically advocate a naturalistic world view (see *More Evidence That Demands a Verdict,* page 3). The label is not used in an invidious sense.

A "COCKSURE COMPLACENCY" OR A "CAREFUL CONSIDERATION"?

Bernard W. Anderson says that "in these days we speak less dogmatically of the 'assured gains' of Biblical Criticism, for someone is just apt to pull the rug out from under our feet." 1/81

About the present need of examining the evidence further, Anderson speaks of "the serious undergraduate himself who may be quite skeptical but is no longer able to dismiss the Bible with cocksure complacency." 1/81

THE CRITICS AND CRITICISM

It seems that every time the term "critic" is used, it denotes a negative discipline or study. That should not be the case. The word critic or criticism is a positive term. A basic definition of criticism is the examination of a problem, a text or issue, etc., to determine its authenticity, reliability or meaning.

For example, Higher Criticism, rightly understood, "is simply the careful scrutiny, on the principles which it is customary to apply to all literature, of the actual phenomena of the Bible, with a view to deduce from these such conclusions as may be warranted regarding the age, authorship, mode of composition, sources, etc., of the different books; and everyone who engages in such inquiries, with whatever aim, is a 'Higher Critic,' and cannot help himself." 2/9 Therefore, anyone who studies the authenticity of a book is a "Higher Critic," whether he is a liberal or a conservative.

The problem that usually leads to a misunderstanding of its use is that High Criticism, as well as other types, has almost exclusively been associated with a "method yielding a certain class of results."

The critical method, so often attached to liberal theology, has been falsely assumed to be strictly a liberal discipline. The various names used for God in Genesis, the similarity of passages in the Synoptic Gospels, etc., are facts to be recognized. This is the job of criticism. The "collation and sifting of evidence, with a view to the obtaining of a satisfactory explanation . . . is a critical process." 2/9

I in no way want to discredit the function of criticism. However, and it shall be apparent in the following pages, I do disagree with the humanistic view that often determines the results of the radical critics. It is the subjective analysis of the critical results with which I take issue. Too many of the objective results are made to coincide with a subjective, rationalistic, anti-supernatural, humanistic outlook.

A DIFFICULT TASK

I realize that when I state a view of radical criticism, it does not necessarily mean that all the radical critics adhere to that particular assumption or view.

It would be impossible, as well as boring, to give all the various views and differences of opinion of the critics on any one problem or assertion. The radical critics, between themselves, differ as much in their assumptions as the conservative scholars often do in their answers.

Each person receiving the early drafts of the manuscript suggested another author or book that should be represented. Finally the line had to be drawn or the work would have gone on *ad infinitum*.

THE PURPOSE

I did not have in mind, nor have I in practice expected, to replace or supersede the use of many excellent works in these fields by very competent biblical and literary scholars.

But much of the research and many of the writings in this book are not available at most secular universities or bookstores. Therefore students, faculty and laymen are often limited in their examination of the subjects dealt with in the classroom and in this book. Some of the best works are unavailable to the student, especially in the area of answers to the radical assumptions.

I will probably be accused of being unfair or lopsided in the presentation of the material in this volume. It will more than likely be said that more space was given to the answers to radical criticism than to its assumptions and their support.

I am of the opinion that the university textbooks and many seminary curriculum are abounding with explanations of the assumptions of radical criticism. However, there seem to be few answers in textbooks (if any, in the majority of them) to these views, especially by capable conservative critics. Perhaps *Daniel in the Critics' Den* will help to offset this imbalance. Thus it will contribute to the process of education.

ATTITUDE

The purpose of this book is not to "kill a critic" or to "destroy a hypothesis," but rather to provide material that can be used to better understand the issues involved and to answer many of the conclusions of the naturalistic critics and their methods. Often I hear various believers incorrectly pass off the radical critics as "infidels" or "blind skeptics."

I am at odds with many of the radical critics over various issues and methods of approach to biblical criticism, but I respect them as individuals and often admire their dedication and research.

The proper motivation behind the use of this book is to glorify and magnify Christ — not to win an argument. Apologetics is not for proving the Word of God but simply for providing a basis for faith.

One should have a gentle and reverent spirit when using this material: "But sanctify Christ as Lord in your hearts, always being ready to make a defense to every one who asks you to give an account for the hope that is in you, yet with gentleness and reverence" (I Peter 3:15).

This material, used with a proper attitude, will help to motivate a person to honestly consider Jesus Christ and will head him toward the central and primary issue — the gospel.

When I share Christ with someone who has some honest doubts, I give him enough apologetics to answer his questions or satisfy his curiosity and then turn the conversation back to his relationship with Christ. The presentation of evidence (apologetics) should never be a substitute for using the Word of God.

A FOIBLE OF SCHOLARSHIP

For years the hackneyed phrases "Daniel didn't write it," "Daniel was a fraud," "Daniel was not written until around 170 B.C.," "Daniel shows many discrepancies," etc., have been heard again and again in the classrooms of our universities and in many seminary and Sunday school curriculum.

Today, it often seems that a theory is accepted because of its place in a textbook and its continued repetition and recognition.

Often repetition is a foible of scholarship. One scholar notes: "Another common and natural phenomenon is the repetition of hypotheses once proposed. As in other fields, so in Bible study, what begins as a very tentative guess becomes by repetition an assumed fact and represents 'the consensus of scholarly opinion.' "

The above should be a warning, not only to the radical critic, but also to the conservative critic.

SOME CRITICISMS

(1) One criticism of my first two books, *Evidence That Demands a Verdict* and *More Evidence That Demands a Verdict* (and it will certainly be made of this book too), has been that the quotes are too long. I have included long quotes so that individuals using the material can better understand the context and, therefore, not misuse a reference. It is easy for quotations to be misleading. I have tried to avoid a misrepresentation of any writer.

(2) Another criticism is that many quotes are very similar and therefore unnecessary. Again my purpose here is to give the person using the material ample sources so that he can choose what he thinks is relevant. Most books have limited documentation and, therefore, if several people use them, they begin to sound like parrots. *Daniel in the Critics' Den* has sufficient sources to allow its use by various people without their sounding like a broken record. Also, it permits those using the material to be creative.

(3) Still another criticism is that some references are used several times. Yes, a few quotes are used two times. The reason for this is that they are appropriate in each situation and aid the reader in understanding the issue.

(4) Others will criticize that I didn't deal with Source Criticism, Historical Criticism and epistemology. The purpose of this book is to clarify the issues and give some practical answers to the questions that students and laymen have asked me over the last five years. It is not to give the pros and cons of the multitudes of problems, questions and schools of criticism.

RESEARCH TEAM MEMBERS

Working with me in compiling this research was a team of three students.

Richard Beckham	Louisiana State University
Don Smedley	Dallas Theological Seminary
Don Stewart	Talbot Theological Seminary

After 10 years of traveling and lecturing in universities, I see a great need for Christian students to invest their lives in research.

Robert Mounce, dean of the Potter College of Arts and Humanities at Western Kentucky University, speaks of the commitment and vision necessary for such an endeavor:

"The task of scholarship is in fact a lowly role which demands tremendous dedication. My own personal feeling is that young men with a gift of conceptualization and perception need to be encouraged to really believe that God can be served in the solitude of one's study surrounded by the fruits of scholarly labor."

WHY COPYRIGHTED?

The reason that these notes have been copyrighted is not to limit their use, but to protect them from misuse and to safeguard the rights of the authors and publishers of the multitude of quotations I have used and documented.

OUTLINE FORM

Because the notes are in outline form and the transitions between various concepts are not extensively written out, the effective use of this material will result as a person spends time thinking through individual sections and developing his own convictions. Thus, it becomes his message and not the parroting of someone else's.

GODISNOWHERE

means

GOD IS NO WHERE? or GOD IS NOW HERE?

The outline structure of the notes can sometimes cause a person to misunderstand an illustration or concept. Be cautious in drawing conclusions one way or another when you do not clearly understand something. Study it further and investigate other sources.

BIBLIOGRAPHY

1. Anderson, Bernard W. "Changing Emphasis in Biblical Criticism." *Journal of Bible and Religion.* Vol. 23, April 1955, pp. 81-88.
2. Orr, James. *The Problem of the Old Testament.* New York: Charles Scribner's Sons, 1917.

EXPLANATION OF GENERAL FORMAT

FOOTNOTES: After each quote there will be two sets of numbers divided by a diagonal (example: 47/21-23). The number to the left of the diagonal is the reference to the source in the bibliography at the end of the book. The number on the right refers to the page or pages where the quote is located in the reference source.

BIBLIOGRAPHY: The entire bibliography is placed at the back of the book.

OUTLINE: I have chosen not to use the traditional method of outlining. Instead I am employing a method that is easy to use in locating specific references in printed notes while lecturing.

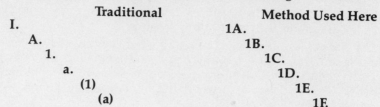

Traditional	Method Used Here
I.	1A.
A.	1B.
1.	1C.
a.	1D.
(1)	1E.
(a)	1F.

INDEXES: Located at the back of the book are two separate indexes to help you in using these notes: 1. Author Index; 2. Subject Index.

BIOGRAPHICAL SKETCHES: At the back of the book is a limited biography of various authors. This will give the reader a background on some of the authors quoted.

chapter 1
Why Is Daniel in the Den?

1A. WHY IS DANIEL IN THE CRITICS' DEN?

1B. Introduction

Daniel has become a focal point of rationalist critics' attacks upon the Old Testament because it contains detailed, accurately fulfilled prophecies which demonstrate their divine inspiration. Because of the author's devotion to God and his great concern for the Jewish people (as shown in Daniel 9 and 10), the Lord seems to have given him a special understanding of what the future held for his people. These prophetic insights extend even to the end time of Hebrew history and the destiny of other nations of the world.

Such amazingly accurate predictions defy the possibility of merely human origin. If these prophecies were composed in the lifetime of the sixth century Daniel, they would compel our acceptance of special revelation from a transcendent, personal God. No anti-supernaturalist position can reasonably be defended if Daniel is a genuine book of prophecy composed in 530 B.C. or in the preceding years.

Therefore, the rationalist scholar is compelled by his self-defense mechanism to seek for some way to avoid the evidential impact of Daniel. The only possible way to evade this testimony is to resort to a theory of spurious composition late enough in history to allow for prior fulfillment of all the "predictions."

Under the influence of ingenious advocates of a second century date hypothesis, the integrity and veracity of the book have been undermined for many students, often involving at the same time a severe loss of faith in the personal God of the Bible. Since a specious type of reasoning has been used as a tool to undermine the faith of many, it becomes necessary to employ a truly sound method of investigation and a responsible handling of the evidence in order to defend the trustworthiness of Daniel and the Bible and to uphold the credibility of maintaining a historical biblical faith.

E. B. Pusey, late Regis Professor of Hebrew and canon of Christ Church, states emphatically:

"The book of Daniel is especially fitted to be a battlefield between faith and unbelief. It admits no half-measures. It is either divine or an imposture. To write any book under the name of another, and to give it out to be his, is, in any case, a forgery, dishonest in itself, and destructive of all trustworthiness. . . . The writer, were he not Daniel, must have lied on a most frightful scale, ascribing to God prophecies which were never uttered, and miracles which are assumed never to have been wrought. In a word, the whole book would be one lie in the Name of God." 31/75

In a similar vein, E. J. Young, late professor of Old Testament at Westminster Theological Seminary, says:

"The book of Daniel purports to be serious history. It claims to be a revelation from the God of heaven which concerns the future welfare of men and nations. If this book were issued at the time of the Maccabees for the purpose of strengthening the faith of the people of that time, and the impression was thereby created that Daniel, a Jew of the 6th century, were the author, then, whether we like it or not, the book is a fraud. There is no escaping this conclusion. It will not do to say that the Jews frequently engaged in such a practice. That does not lessen their guilt one whit. It is one thing to issue a harmless romance under a pseudonym; it is an entirely different thing to issue under a pseudonym a book claiming to be a revelation of God and having to do with the conduct of men and to regard such a book as canonical. The Jews of the inter-testamental period may have done the first; there is no evidence that they ever did the second." 51/25

If the critical views of Daniel are accepted and followed, E. L. Curtis says "that it will appear to some to destroy its religious value and render it unworthy of a place within the Sacred Canon." 52/555 And this is exactly how, in point of fact, radical criticism has affected the attitude of many Bible students toward the Book of Daniel.

Now it should be clearly understood that even a partial acceptance of this radical theory concerning the composition of Daniel carries with it grave implications as to the foundations of the Christian faith. The authority of Christ Himself is fatally compromised by this late date hypothesis.

In Matthew 24, the Olivet Discourse, Christ gave His own list of events of the end time. As a part of this chronology of future events, He explicitly referred to the prophecy of Daniel (the "abomination of desolation" passage in 9:27; 11:31; 12:11). But beyond this one clear reference it is also vitally significant that interspersed throughout the Gospels are Christ's references to

Himself as the Son of Man. Nowhere in the Gospels is this illustrated more graphically than in Matthew, where clear references to Daniel's vision of the Son of Man (Daniel 7:9-14,22) are made repeatedly (Matthew 16:27,28; 19:28; 24:27-31; 25:31 ff.; 26:64) along with many more references to the power and authority of the Son of Man. There can be no doubt, from all these references to Daniel's Son of Man vision, that Christ clearly viewed it as authentic prophecy referring to Himself.

Now if Christ were mistaken about the Book of Daniel, then He must also have been mistaken about His own identity. And if this be so, it follows that the Christian faith may be called into question. At stake is the very trustworthiness of Christ's statements concerning our own faith and salvation through Him.

These two issues are inextricably involved with each other. If Daniel is authentic prophecy and its recorded visions are accurate descriptions of the future given by God Himself, then Christ's view of it and of Himself are true. But if the book is a fraud, then Christ was mistaken concerning it, and much of the basis for our faith in His integrity and authority must come under severe questioning.

B. K. Waltke points out: "Jesus Christ regarded the book as a prophetic preview of future history, and, indeed, of the divine program for a future that still lies ahead (Matthew 24:4 ff., Mark 13:5 ff., Luke 21:8 ff.). If He is wrong in His interpretation of the book then He must be less than an omniscient, inerrant God incarnate. On the other hand, if His appraisal is right, then we cannot question His claim to deity in this regard." 74/320

The reliability of much of Scripture depends upon the reliability of Daniel. (Compare II Timothy 3:16; II Peter 1:20,21; Luke 21:27; and Mark 13:26, just to name a few, with Daniel 7:13; 9:27; 11:31; 12:11.) Daniel's reliability is also important because of the prophecies it contains.

According to William Newell: "If the keys of the Bible, up to the book of Psalms, hang on Moses' books, those of the rest of the Bible, through Revelation, hang on Daniel; and indeed very many of the prophetic Psalms fail to open to us till we see their solution in the wonderful visions of the faithful seer of the captivity." 53/315

And as Erwin Jenkins points out: "The best proof for the inspiration of the Scripture is prophecy. But because the professing church has allowed false teachers to come in, prophecy has been neglected and laid aside as untenable. When this is done the people fall prey to every wind of doctrine, eventually disbelieving that the Bible is the Word of God. Prophecy is the most sturdy rung in the ladder of the Christian faith." 21/5

Also concerning the importance of Daniel in relation to the integrity of the Scriptures, B. K. Waltke states: "If the book contains true predictions, then there is firm reason to believe that this book ultimately owes its origin to One who can predict the future; on the contrary, if it is a spurious, fraudulent, although well intentioned, piece of literature, then the reliability of other books in the canon of Scripture may legitimately be questioned." 74/320

A. C. Gaebelein says this about those who reject prophecy: "They rather listen to the theories or dreams of the human mind than to God's plan, how He is going to bring this earth to a knowledge of Himself. Thousands of fortune tellers, astrologers, demon possessed mediums, who ask the dead, make a fine living throughout Christendom and profit greatly by the desire of thousands to know a little about the future. And here in the Bible God has uncovered the future, but few of His people pay any attention to it." 54/2

Allis also remarks: "In textbooks which represent the critical or higher critical viewpoint it is regarded as a matter of prime importance to explain the supernatural, which often means to explain it away, and to deal with the Bible in such a way that the supernatural will really cease to be supernatural. The seriousness of this attempt cannot be exaggerated." 78/1

2B. The Problem

Because of the prophetic nature of Daniel, it has been attacked on every possible ground by many proponents of higher critical theories, that is, by men who assume from the outset that the supernatural is impossible. Thus, they contend that anything appearing or claiming to be miraculous must be discounted as fictitious or somehow be explained away by natural causes. Therefore, any predictive prophecy Daniel contains must be discredited and explained by naturalistic means. Consequently the scholars have come to the conclusion that Daniel must be a historical fiction written by someone in the Maccabean period (the early second century B.C.). They attempt to undermine the integrity of the author by showing that he has an erroneous knowledge of history and confuses fact with fiction. This they regard to be proof positive that the book was concocted four centuries later than the events it relates.

3B. The Radical Method

These critics attempt to uncover a pattern of inaccuracy and contradiction or confusion pervading the entire Book of Daniel. Their goal in so doing is to discredit the veracity of virtually all of the historical records in the book.

At this point it is well to observe that we know relatively little about the details of ancient history and that what we do know ought to be asserted with some caution. It is a wise procedure in the analysis of any serious work of ancient literature to consider it authentic until proven fraudulent. In other words, the initial presumption should be that the ancient document is trustworthy until it is proven erroneous.

Now the rationalist higher critics show a consistent tendency to operate on the opposite assumption in regard to biblical books: They are assumed to be spurious, fallacious and error-ridden unless or until corroborative evidence comes from secular sources. This is the critics' method with Daniel. It is very important to note that such opinions of the anti-supernaturalist critics are generally stated with all confidence. Notice also that in the course of the critics' deductions, they seem to assume a completely adequate grasp of all the relevant data of the remote past, whereas they suppose the ancient writer lacked adequate knowledge of his own times. Such scholars also maintain that some of the authors actually wrote later than the period which their books describe. They claim the words and style of the book point to a later period (*e.g.*, the Greek words in Daniel).

4B. Purpose of This Writing

In the course of this writing, the arguments of these critics will be examined. The method will be as follows:

1. To state the problem.
2. To present statements by the critics adequately representing the critical view.
3. To assess the radical critical view for actual content.
4. To examine the actual text being attacked.
5. To examine the evidence bearing on the arguments.

While reading this book, remember that the questions posed by the radical critics involve the text of Daniel. Most of their contentions can be adequately refuted by a careful examination of the text itself — of the actual content and what it says.

J. D. Wilson states: "Many suppose that the questions involved are exceedingly recondite and can be approached only by learned Orientalists, and so they shrink from personal investigation; but there is nothing mysterious in the question of the date of the Book of Daniel. Common sense and honest judgment provide all the equipment for examining the case from top to bottom. Scholarship will but verify the verdict which good sense shall render." 43/14

5B. History of Radical Criticism

Erwin Jenkins writes, "The Book of Daniel has been accepted as genuine by the Jews and also the Christian church up to the third century. No one doubted its authenticity until the enemy of Christianity, the Neo-Platonist, Porphyry, wrote a treatise against its validity. Porphyry not only rejected the historicity of Daniel but all the sacred books of the Old and New Testaments. Porphyry's arguments were based on his antitheistic philosophical presuppositions. He said that prophecy was impossible and, therefore, Daniel could not have spoken such." 21/8,9

Later, as Professor Young (*An Introduction to the Old Testament*) relates: "*Uriel Acosta* (1590-1647), a Jewish rationalist, considered the book of Daniel to have been forged for the purpose of favoring the doctrine of the resurrection of the body. In 1727 the English deist, *Anthony Collins*, in an appendix to his work "Scheme of Literal Prophecy Considered," attacked the integrity of the prophecy. But probably the earliest carefully wrought out attack on Daniel was made by *Leonhard Bertholdt* (1806-08)." 50/354

In his *Introduction to the Old Testament*, R. K. Harrison brings us up to date: "The German literary-critical movement seized avidly upon the supposition that the prophecy could contain no predictive element, and repudiated the Jewish and Christian tradition of a sixth-century B.C. date of composition for the book, despite the arguments of some conservative scholars. Objections to the historicity of Daniel were copied uncritically from book to book, and by the second decade of the twentieth century no scholar of general liberal background who wished to preserve his academic reputation either dared or desired to challenge the current critical trend. Since this position was obviously of great importance to those who maintained it, some appraisal of its principles and contents may well be desirable." 19/1111

The influence of Porphyry upon the critics is unquestionable; following his approach, they regarded all biblical prophecy as mere forthtelling rather than foretelling. However, not all of the critics were able to accept this position, that prophecy had no predictive element. Some authorities among the critics, such as Ackerman, Gunkel and Quillaume, had reservations, for even a passing look at the Hebrew prophets reveals the absurdity of the idea that they did not refer to events in the distant future.

Harrison continues: "As Rowley has pointedly remarked in this connection, the common modern antithesis between foretelling and forthtelling would have had little meaning for the ancient Israelites, since the prophets were commonly engaged in predicting the future, frequently as it arose from contemporary happenings, though by no means exclusively so." 19/1112

6B. Admission of Dr. Driver

Dr. S. R. Driver, the English scholar, was one of the foremost radical critics. He states: ". . . the age and authorship of the books of the Old Testament can be determined (so far as this is possible) only upon the basis of the internal evidence supplied by the books themselves . . . no external evidence worthy of credit exists." 12/xi

In spite of this statement, Driver follows it with external evidence to support 11 pages of historical and philological reasons why Daniel could not have been written in the sixth century B.C. 45/42

Says Professor R. D. Wilson: "The most admirable thing about Doctor Driver, and that which gained for him his exalted position in the scholarly world, was the masterly manner with which he essayed to support his judgments based upon the internal evidence of a book by evidence external to the book itself. What I object to in the case of Doctor Driver and his followers, is that they seem to seek in every possible way to pervert the internal and external evidence as to the Canon in general, and as to the canonicity and date of Daniel in particular, so as to confirm their own preconceived opinion as to what they ought to be." 45/42

7B. Content

The focus of this writing deals with the historical Book of Daniel, contained in the Old Testament of the Christian Scriptures. A simple outline of Daniel follows:

Chapter

1 Nebuchadnezzar carries the finest, most intelligent youths off to Babylon

   Daniel and his three friends refuse the king's meat and wine

   Daniel and his three friends are wiser than all others in the kingdom

2 Daniel tells the king what his dream was and what it meant: prophetic content

   Daniel is appointed the ruler over all wise men of Babylon

3 Daniel's three friends are thrown in a fiery furnace for not bowing to the image of Nebuchadnezzar

4 Daniel interprets Nebuchadnezzar's dream of being like a beast

5 Daniel interprets the handwriting on the wall for Belshazzar

   Daniel is made the chief official of Babylonian provinces under Darius the Mede

6 Daniel is saved from the den of lions

7   Daniel's dream — first year of Belshazzar — of the four
    kingdoms; the final kingdom; the antichrist

8   Daniel's dream — third year of Belshazzar — of the
    Medo-Persian empire; the Grecian empire; four separate
    kingdoms; the antichrist

9   Daniel's dream — first year of Darius — of the 70 weeks and
    the Messiah's 69 weeks

10-12 Daniel's dream — third year of Cyrus — of four kings; a
       mighty king; four kingdoms; the kings of north and south;
       the time of the end; the antichrist

The first part of Daniel deals with historical narratives, which
include some miraculous elements; the last part, from chapter 7
on, deals with dreams and visions of future events.

8B. Summary

A reading of the Book of Daniel reveals that he was a man of great
integrity who had the divine gift of interpreting prophetic
dreams. The book records miraculous events in Daniel's life and
includes several remarkable prophecies, most of which are
centered around the coming of the Messiah and the end of our
present era. Rationalist critics feel compelled to regard the
miraculous elements as wholly fictitious and consider the
prophetic elements to be largely fraudulent, having been
composed after the fulfillment, in every case, of successful
prediction.

The critics' theories tend to assume external discrepancies (*i.e.*,
the book does not agree with certain secular historical sources),
and they charge the book with various flaws and inconsistencies.
As committed opponents to the supernatural, they are forced to
find flaws in as many places as possible throughout Daniel in
order that they might destroy the author's reputation for
truthfulness and integrity. In so doing they pave the way for the
humanistic theory that it was written in the reign of Antiochus
Epiphanes around 176 B.C. Their purpose is to prove that Daniel
is inaccurate not only with respect to its prophecies but also in
some of its references to Epiphanes himself.

Of course it must follow that if the critics can prove their case,
then they have seriously undermined the credibility of Christ, the
Bible and the Christian faith. But if, on the other hand, the
arguments of the critics are shown to be ill-founded and
untenable, not reconcilable with the historical evidence, then
another important facet of the Bible and the Christian faith will
have withstood the attempts of skeptics to discredit it.

chapter 2
Daniel Can Withstand
the Critics

2A. POSITIVE EVIDENCE

Before entering the maze of critical arguments, I will present some of
the positive evidence for the authenticity of Daniel in order to show
that even before a single critical objection is raised, a massive
amount of evidence exists concerning the authenticity and integrity
of the book.

1B. Archaeological Evidence

If Daniel is authentic, then it is essential that it be accurate in its
historical details.

1C. ACCURACY CONCERNING BABYLONIAN HISTORY

The historical accuracy of the author regarding Babylonian
history makes it difficult to believe the book was written some
400 years after its historical setting. As Raven asserts, Daniel's
accurate representation of history in Babylon shows that it
must have been written there. 32/331

Ira Price, a liberal critic, admits that Daniel 4:30 gives a true
picture of Nebuchadnezzar's building activities.29/302,303

Another example of historical detail is the story of Darius
ordering Daniel thrown into the lions' den. If the book were
written in 168 B.C., how did the author know that Darius the
Mede was a fire worshiper and would not have thrown Daniel
into the fire, as did Nebuchadnezzar to Daniel's friends? It is
remarkable that in all the details of the book no historical error
has *ever* been proven. 33/331

Among the historical details recorded in the Book of Daniel are
the threats to the Chaldeans of being dismembered and their
houses made a rubbish heap (2:5) and to all who disobey the
king's decree of being burned alive (3:6) or thrown into the
lions' den (6:7). Then there are the references to men's dress
(3:21) and to women's participation at the royal banquets (5:3).
Note also the practice of mentioning first the Medes, then the
Persians (6:8,12,15). In the time described by the Book of

Esther, Persians usually were listed first (Esther 1:3,14,18,19). A forger of the Maccabean period could not have known such details and would have committed at least a few anachronistic mistakes, nor could he have known it was impossible — even for the king — to change a law of the Medes and Persians once it had been promulgated (Daniel 6:8,12,15). 20/10

W. F. Albright, the great Semitic scholar, states: "We may safely expect the Babylonian Jewish author to be acquainted with the main facts of the Neo-Babylonian history." 60/113

2C. ACCURACY CONCERNING NEBUCHADNEZZAR

Nebuchadnezzar's vision is given in Daniel 4 and ends with, "This matter is by the decree of the watchers, and the demand by the word of the holy ones: to the intent that the living may know that the most High ruleth in the kingdom of men, and giveth it to whomsoever He will, and *setteth up over it the basest of men*" (4:17, KJV). These last words are a remarkable reference to Nebuchadnezzar's humble family origin. This lowly origin was otherwise unknown until the discovery of an inscription made by his father, Nabopolassar. 4/89-91

The inscription states: "Nabopolassar, the just king, the shepherd called of Merodach, the offspring of Nin-menna, great and illustrious queen of queens, holding the hand of Nebo and Tasmit, the prince the beloved of Ea am I. When I *in my littleness, the son of a nobody*, sought faithfully after the sacred places of Nebo and Merodach, my lords: when my mind pondered how to establish their decrees, and to complete their abodes, and my ears were opened to justice and righteousness: when Merodach who knows the hearts of the gods of heaven and earth, who sees the ways of men most clearly, had perceived the intention of *me, the insignificant, who among men was not visible*, and in the land where I was born had designed me for the chieftainship and for the rulership of the land and people over whom I was nominated, and had sent a good genius to go at my side: when he had prospered all that I had done, and had sent Nergal, strongest of the gods, to go beside me — He subdued my foes, dashed in pieces my enemies: — the Assyrian, who from the days of old ruled over all men, *I, the weak, the feeble*, in dependence on the lord of lords, in the strong might of Nebo and Merodach my lords, held back their feet from the land of Akkad and broke their yoke." 4/90; 25/57

In this inscription Nabopolassar reveals that he was not of royal birth, "the son of a nobody" (an expression found in Assyrian inscriptions to signify non-royal birth). He also indicates that he was not important in social circles by describing himself as

"the insignificant," "not visible," "the weak" and "the feeble."
This is the kind of knowledge — the lowly origin of Babylon's
greatest king — which succeeding generations soon must have
forgotten, and therefore it constitutes strong evidence for the
historical accuracy of Daniel. 4/89-91

Boutflower writes: ". . . such resemblances of style between
the utterances of the Nebuchadnezzar of the monuments and
the Nebuchadnezzar of Holy Scripture form part of the
cumulative evidence in favour of the authenticity of the Book of
Daniel. For we may well question whether a Jewish writer of
the age of the Maccabees would be acquainted with the literary
style of the scribes of the New Babylonian empire, or with the
strong poetic tendencies of the real Nebuchadnezzar." 4/104

Concerning such a hypothetical author, Boutflower asks: "Is it
likely . . . that such a writer would be aware of the humble
origin of this great king, of his deep religiousness, his intense
devotion to his beloved Babylon, his fondness for great
occasions, his love of splendour and display, his partiality, not
only for the pleasures of the chase but also for the woodman's
art? Could we expect him to be so exactly informed as to the
ideal of a prosperous world-wide empire centred at Babylon
which formed the aim of this monarch? Would he be likely to
picture as a prince of peace one who in the other Scriptures
appears rather as a man of war? Yet as to all these particulars,
which may be gleaned from the contemporary Babylonian
records, the writer of this Book is seen to be perfectly informed.
Are we not, then, justified in regarding the Book of Daniel as
genuine history, rather than as a religious romance, the work of
a later age?" 4/104

Corresponding to Nebuchadnezzar's boast (Daniel 4:30) of
building Babylon, Free states: "The East India House
inscription, now in London, has six columns of Babylonian
writing telling of the stupendous building operations which
the king carried on in enlarging and beautifying Babylon."
14/228

Barton quotes an inscription of Nebuchadnezzar's which bears
an amazing correspondence to Daniel 4:30. "The fortifications
of Esagila and Babylon I strengthened and established the
name of my reign forever." 70/479

From the critical point of view, it is not easy to explain how a
late author would know that Babylon's greatness in the early
sixth century was due to Nebuchadnezzar. But if the author
wrote the book around 532 B.C., this becomes perfectly
understandable. 14/229

3C.   KNOWLEDGE OF BELSHAZZAR

Knowledge of Belshazzar seems to have disappeared by the time of Herodotus (*c.* 450 B.C.). This indicates that the author of Daniel knew more about the sixth century B.C. than would have been possible for a second century writer. 3/371; *cf.* 11/200

J. D. Wilson quotes Kuenen: "I am certain, after much examination, that the writer of the Book of Daniel shows a most intimate personal acquaintance with the palace of Nebuchadnezzar and the affairs of the Babylonian Court and Empire, and that the book was written during the exile." 43/88,89

Wilson also quotes Lenormant: "The more I read and reread Daniel, the more I am struck with the truth of the tableaux of the Babylonian Court traced in the first six chapters. Whoever is not the slave of preconceived opinions must confess when comparing these with the cuneiform monuments that they are really ancient and written but a short distance from the Courts themselves." 43/89

Wilson himself asserts: "No Jew whose people had been living for centuries under Persian and Grecian rule could relate with such unconscious simplicity the actual condition of affairs in Babylon 370 years before his own time." 43/91

Archer maintains that because of the historical accuracy of Daniel, critics have dated considerable portions of the book 100 years or more before the Maccabean revolt. This tends to weaken their late date theory. 3/402.

Several of the historical episodes recorded in Daniel show the pagan government treating the Jews favorably. Thus the reason for their inclusion in a book designed especially to encourage a people persecuted by a foreign government (as were the Jews of the second century B.C.) is unexplainable.

In the *New Bible Dictionary*, J. E. Whitcomb, Jr., concludes: "On the basis of a careful comparison of the cuneiform evidence concerning Belshazzar with the statements of the fifth chapter of Daniel, R. P. Dougherty concluded that the view that the fifth chapter of Daniel originated in the Maccabean age is discredited (*op. cit.*, p. 200). But the same conclusion must be reached concerning the fourth and sixth chapters of Daniel as well, as we have pointed out above. Therefore, since the critics are almost unanimous in their admission that the Book of Daniel is the product of one author (*cf.* R. H. Pfeiffer. *op. cit.*, pp. 761,762), we may safely assert that the book could not possibly have been written as late as the Maccabean age." 69/291,292

2B. Fulfilled Prophecy

If Daniel is authentic, then its prophetic sections should accurately describe the events they foretell.

1C. PROPHECY OF THE 70 WEEKS

In Daniel 9:24-27, a prophecy is given in three specific parts concerning the Messiah. The first part states that at the end of 69 weeks, the Messiah will come to Jerusalem. (Actually the 7 and 62 weeks are understood as 69 seven-year periods. For the explanation see Hoehner, 73/117 ff.) The starting point of the 69 weeks is the decree to restore and rebuild Jerusalem.

The second part states that after the Messiah comes, He will be cut off (idiom for His death as well as not being able to rule His kingdom). Then the prince to come will destroy Jerusalem and the temple.

All of the above, according to Daniel 9:24-26, takes place *after* the 69 weeks of years. But Daniel 9:24 mentions 70 weeks (7+62+1), not just 69. The final week is described in 9:27. Many scholars believe 9:27 discusses a different person and time than that of 9:26. Even though the author refers to the prince, the reference is probably to another prince who is to come later in history. (Double references are somewhat common in prophecy. For example, a reference, such as Genesis 49:10, may point to King David and also later to Christ.) This is supported by their actions. The prince in 9:27 forces Jewish temple practices to stop, but the prince in 9:26 has just destroyed the temple! So probably the prince in 9:27 comes later after the temple is rebuilt, an event which is yet to occur. Anyway, no matter which way one interprets the 70th week (the last seven years of the prophecy), the overall prophecy can still be examined historically. For further study on this prophecy in Daniel see *Chronological Aspects of the Life of Christ* (73). The rationalistic critics begin the *terminus a quo* (beginning) of the prophecy 490 years before 168 B.C., since they believe this is all prophecy after the events, or else they say that the 70 weeks are merely symbolic and furnish no basis for computation.

Concerning the first part of the prophecy (the coming of the Messiah), Wilson explains: "Included in the prophecy of the Seventy Weeks is the specific prediction that from the going forth of a commandment to restore and build Jerusalem unto Messiah the Prince, there would be sixty-nine weeks. Those weeks are weeks of years. After four hundred and eighty-three years Messiah was to come." 43/139

1D. The Text

Daniel 9:24 "Seventy weeks have been decreed for your
people and your holy city, to finish the
transgression, to make an end of sin, to make
atonement for iniquity, to bring in everlasting
righteousness, to seal up vision and prophecy,
and to anoint the most holy place.

25 "So you are to know and discern that from the
issuing of a decree to restore and rebuild
Jerusalem until Messiah the Prince there will be
seven weeks and sixty-two weeks; it will be built
again, with plaza and moat, even in times of
distress.

26 "Then after the sixty-two weeks the Messiah will
be cut off and have nothing, and the people of
the prince who is to come will destroy the city
and the sanctuary. And its end will come with a
flood; even to the end there will be war;
desolations are determined.

27 "And he will make a firm covenant with the
many for one week, but in the middle of the
week he will put a stop to sacrifice and grain
offering; and on the wing of abominations will
come one who makes desolate, even until a
complete destruction, one that is decreed, is
poured out on the one who makes desolate."

2D. Interpretation of the Prophecy

  1E. Main features of this prophecy (taken from Dr. James
Rosscup's class notes, Talbot Theological Seminary,
California)

  Concerns Daniel's people, Israel, and Daniel's city,
Jerusalem (9:24)

  Two princes mentioned
   1. Messiah (9:25)
   2. Prince to come (9:26)

  Time period of 70 weeks (9:24)
   1. As a unit (9:24)
   2. As a division of three periods: 7 weeks, 62 weeks, and
     1 week (9:25,27)

  Specified beginning of the 70 weeks (9:25)

  Messiah appears at end of 69 weeks (9:25)

  Destruction of city and sanctuary by people of prince to
come (9:26)

Covenant made firm between Israel and the coming prince at the beginning of last week (9:27); this covenant is broken mid-week (9:27)

At end of the 70 weeks, Israel will have everlasting righteousness (9:24)

2E. Time measure indicated by 70 weeks

Jewish concept of week

1. The Hebrew word for "week" is *shabua* and literally means a "seven." (We should disassociate any English concept of week with the concept intended by Gabriel.) Then, in Hebrew, the idea of 70 weeks is "seventy sevens."

2. The Jews were familiar with a "seven" of both days and years. "It was, in certain respects, even more important" (Alva J. McClain, *Daniel's Prophecy of the Seventy Weeks*, p. 13).

3. Leviticus 25:2-4 illustrates the above fact. Leviticus 25:8 shows that there was a multiple of a week of years.

Remembering what has been said previously, there are several reasons for believing that the 70 weeks mentioned in Daniel are 70 sevens of years.

1. Daniel had been thinking in terms of years and multiples of seven earlier in the chapter (Daniel 9:1,2).

2. Daniel knew that the Babylonian captivity was based on violation of the Sabbatic year, and since they were in captivity for 70 years, evidently the Sabbatic year was violated 490 years (Leviticus 26:32-35; II Chronicles 36:21 and Daniel 9:24).

3. The context is consistent and makes sense when we understand the 70 weeks as years.

4. *Shabua* is found in Daniel 10:2,3. Context demands it to mean "weeks" of days. It is literally "three sevens of days." If Daniel meant days in 9:24-27, why don't we find the same form of expression as that in chapter 10? Obviously, years are meant in chapter 9.

3E. Length of prophetic year

The calendar year used in the Scriptures must be determined from the Scriptures themselves.

1. Historically — Compare Genesis 7:11 with Genesis 8:4 and the two of these with Genesis 7:24 and Genesis 8:3.

2. Prophetically — Many scriptures refer to the great
   tribulation under various terms, but all have a
   common denominator of a 360-day year.

   Daniel 9:27 — "Midst" of the 70th week (obviously
   three and a half years)
   Daniel 7:24,25 — "a time and times and the dividing of
   time" (literally three and a half times)
   Revelation 13:4-7 — "forty and two months" (three
   and a half years)
   Revelation 12:13,14 — "a time and times and half a
   time"
   Revelation 12:6 — "a thousand two hundred and three
   score days" (1,260 days or three and a half years)

4E.   Beginning of 70 weeks

Several commandments or decrees in Israel's history have
been suggested as the *terminus a quo* of the 483 years. These
are:

1. The decree of Cyrus, 539 B.C. (Ezra 1:1-4).
2. The decree of Darius, 519-518 B.C. (Ezra 5:3-7).
3. The decree of Artaxerxes to Ezra, 457 B.C. (Ezra
   7:11-16).
4. The decree of Artaxerxes to Nehemiah, 444 B.C.
   (Nehemiah 2:1-8). 73/121ff.

However, the one which best fits the data is number four,
the decree of Artaxerxes to Nehemiah. (Archer prefers the
starting point being the decree of Artaxerxes in the
seventh year in 457 B.C. 3/401 *Cf.* Finegan, *Handbook of
Biblical Chronology,* Princeton, 1964, pp. 294-298.)

J. D. Wilson comments on the starting point of the
prophecy: "The next decree is referred to in Neh. ii. It was
in the twentieth year of Artaxerxes. The words of the
decree are not given, but its subject matter can easily be
determined. Nehemiah hears of the desolate condition of
Jerusalem. He is deeply grieved. The King asks the reason.
Nehemiah replies 'the city, the place of my fathers'
sepulchres lieth waste and the gates thereof are consumed
with fire.' The King bids him make request. He does so
promptly, asking an order from the King that 'I be sent to
the city that I may build it.' And, as we read, he was sent,
and he rebuilt Jerusalem.

"This decree then is the 'commandment to restore and
rebuild Jerusalem.' There is no other decree authorizing
the restoration of the city. This decree authorizes the

restoration and the book of Nehemiah tells how the work was carried on. The exigencies of their various theories have led men to take some other decree for the *terminus a quo* of their calculations, but it is not apparent how any could have done so without misgivings. This decree of Neh. ii is the commandment to restore and rebuild Jerusalem; no other decree gives any permission to restore the city. All other decrees refer to the building of the temple and the temple only." 43/141,142

Wilson then gives the length of the year used in the calculation of the 483 years. "The only years whose length is given in the Bible are of 360 days — twelve months of 30 days each. Gen. vii, 11, viii, 3-4; Rev. xi, 2-3, xii, 6, xiii, 5. It seems not unreasonable to take the period designed as 360 days. In that case the 483d year from [444] B.C. is [33] A.D., the date of the Crucifixion."* 43/143

*Note: The dates I have used in this work are from the most recent scholarship. When older sources with unlikely dates are quoted, the correct dates are set in to avoid confusion. The dates quoted in this work are from H. W. Hoehner's *Chronological Aspects of the Life of Christ*. Hoehner has thoroughly researched this issue, including careful scrutiny of Robert Anderson's *The Coming Prince*. Therefore, for a complete explanation of the dating, see Hoehner's work (73).

If Daniel is correct, the time from the edict to restore and rebuild Jerusalem (Nisan 1, 444 B.C.) to the coming of the Messiah to Jerusalem is 483 years, each year equaling the 360-day year (173,880 days). Will these calculations match with history and time?

3D. Day of Christ's Crucifixion

Hoehner demonstrates that the only logical day for Christ's crucifixion is Nisan 14, A.D. 33, or according to our calendar, April 3, A.D. 33. See chapters IV and V of Hoehner's *Chronological Aspects of the Life of Christ*.

4D. Calculation of 69 Weeks

Using the 360-day year, Hoehner calculates the terminal day of the 69 weeks of Daniel's prophecy as follows: "Multiplying the sixty-nine weeks by seven years for each week by 360 days gives a total of 173,880 days. The difference between 444 B.C. and A.D. 33 then is 476 solar years. By multiplying 476 by 365.24219879 or by 365 days, 5 hours, 48 minutes, 45.975 seconds, one comes to 173,855 days, 6 hours, 52 minutes, 44 seconds, or 173,855 days. This leaves only 25 days to be accounted for between 444 B.C. and A.D. 33. By adding the 25 days to March 5 (of 444 B.C.), one comes to March 30 (of A.D. 33) which was Nisan 10 in A.D. 33. This is the triumphal entry of Jesus into Jerusalem." 73/138

The terminal event of the 69 weeks is the presentation of Christ Himself to Israel as the Messiah as predicted in Zechariah 9:9. This materialized on Monday, Nisan 10 (March 30), A.D. 33. On the following Friday, April 3, A.D. 33, Christ was crucified or "cut off" (Daniel 9:26).

After the termination of the 69 weeks and before the commencement of the 70th week, two events had to occur:

(1) The "cutting off" of the Messiah.

(2) The destruction of the city and temple.

The temple was destroyed in A.D. 70 by Titus the Roman. Therefore, according to Daniel's prophecy, the Messiah had to come and be crucified between March 30, A.D. 33 and A.D. 70. Christ was crucified April 3, A.D. 33.

The following is a chart of the prophetic calculations using the prophetic year of 360 days:

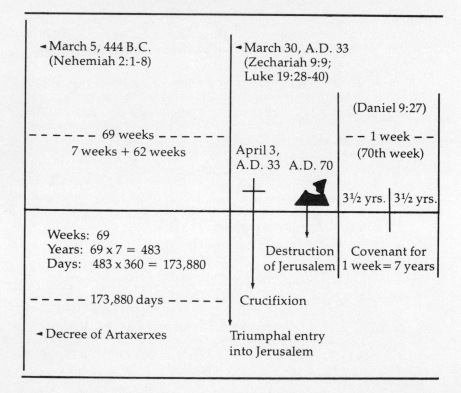

Verification of the prophetic calculations using our calendar (Julian):

    a. 444 B.C. to A.D. 33 is 476 yrs.
        (444 plus 33 is 477, but 1 B.C.
        to A.D. 1 is 1 year and not two.
        One must subtract 1 year from 477.)

b. 476 yrs. x 365.24219879 days =	173,855 days
c. March 5 to March 30 =	25 days
	173,880 days

Wilson discusses the second part of the prophecy after the Messiah's death (Nisan 14, four days after His triumphal entry), when the prince was to come and destroy Jerusalem and the temple (sanctuary). This actually happened when Titus destroyed the city in A.D. 70.

"After that, the Roman prince sent an army which utterly destroyed the city and temple of Jerusalem. That destruction was complete. The temple was not simply polluted, as it was by Antiochus Epiphanes — it was destroyed. It has not been reared in Jerusalem since. The Jewish ritual was ended. It has never been restored, and it never can be. It has had no priesthood since Jerusalem fell; for every son of Aaron was slain. There can be no more priestly sacrifices, nor atonement by high priest; for in that dire disaster, the older covenant passed away. Its vitality and validity had ceased when the Lamb of God was offered upon Calvary; but for forty years the outward shell remained. That shell was removed in the destruction of Jerusalem, 70 A.D." 43/149

So Daniel prophesies accurately concerning the Messiah in his prophecy of the 70 weeks. Even if the 165 B.C. date of authorship is correct, these events take place at least 200 years later during the time of Christ. They include:

1. The coming of the Messiah.
2. The death of the Messiah.

3. The destruction of Jerusalem and the temple.

The third part of the prophecy pertaining to the 70th week is yet to occur.

2C. PROPHECY OF ROME

Another accurate prophecy concerns Rome. The critics' attempt to discredit it is weak.

Archer sets forth the case: "It is fair to say that the weakest spot in the whole structure of the Maccabean theory is to be found in the identification of the fourth empire predicted in chapter 2. In order to maintain their position, the late-date theorists have to interpret this fourth empire as referring to the kingdom of the Macedonians or Greeks founded by Alexander the Great around 330 B.C. This means that the third empire must be identified with the Persian realm established by Cyrus the Great, and the second empire has to be the short-lived Median power briefly maintained by the legendary Darius the Mede. According to this interpretation, then, the head of gold in chapter 2 represents the Chaldean empire, the breast of silver the Median empire, the belly and the thighs of brass the Persian empire, and the legs of iron the Greek empire. Although this identification of the four empires is widely held by scholars today, it is scarcely tenable in the light of internal evidence." 3/396,97

There is no evidence that Daniel considered the Medes and the Persians separate empires at the time Babylon was conquered, while there is strong evidence that he considered Medo-Persia an integrated union, composing one empire.

The interpretation of the vision in Daniel 8 expressly states that the ram with two horns represents the kings of Media and Persia (8:20). The shaggy male goat with a prominent horn that tramples on the ram represents the kingdom of Greece, and the large horn is the first king (8:21), which clearly refers to Alexander the Great.

From a reading of the text, it is obvious the author of Daniel considered Medo-Persia one empire. The ram's longer horn (cf. 8:3) coming up last corresponds to history: Media was a strong empire with Persia under its dominance until the Persians under Cyrus rose in power and subdued the other parts of the pre-existing Median empire.

Therefore, a Median empire predated the Medo-Persian empire and co-existed with the Babylonian empire. But Daniel was not concerned with the Median empire because it never ruled Israel.

Also, when Daniel interprets *peres* (5:28), the last word written on the wall, he clearly points to the Persian empire as the one coming to defeat the Chaldeans. The word *peres* is derived from the verb *peras* and is a word play meaning "to divide, separate." But it also specifically indicates "Persia." This clearly connotes that Persia will overtake Chaldea. This is one of the strongest arguments of all and makes identification of the fourth kingdom with Rome absolutely compelling.

In addition, Archer points to Daniel's dream in chapter 7 to support the Babylon, Medo-Persia, Greece and Rome interpretation. The first figure is a lion, which all scholars agree represents Babylon. The second figure, a bear, best represents the Medo-Persian empire — the three ribs that it devours correspond accurately with the empire's major conquests of Lydia, Babylon and Egypt. The third figure, a four-headed leopard, represents Greece because Greece was divided into four kingdoms after Alexander's death. The fourth figure, a beast with 10 horns, corresponds to the two legs of iron and feet of iron and clay of the statue in chapter 2. This beast fits well as the Roman empire. The legs suggest the two separate empires formed under Diocletian, and iron, the strongest of the metals, illustrates Rome, the strongest of the kingdoms. 3/383.

Archer concludes: "From the standpoint of the symbolism of chapters 2, 7 and 8, therefore, the identification of the four empires with Babylon, Medo-Persia, Greece and Rome presents a perfect correspondence, whereas the identifications involved in the Maccabean date theory present the gravest problems and discrepancies." 3/397,398

The critics' strongest argument for identifying Daniel's fourth empire with Alexander and his Greek successors is derived from the appearances of the little horns in chapters 7 and 8. They make the superfluous deduction that both little horns represent the same individual.

However, a glance at the text shows the fallaciousness of this assumption. The little horn of chapter 7 develops out of the 10 horns of the terrible beast representing the fourth empire. This little horn pulls out three of the 10 horns.

In contrast, the little horn of chapter 8 develops after the male goat's large horn has been broken and replaced by four horns. Obviously these are disparate representations, by no means intended to represent the same kingdom, king or situation. Only the most obdurate and logic-stretching preconceptions enable the critics to equate these two little horns.

Archer comments: ". . . the four-winged leopard of chapter 7 clearly corresponds to the four-horned goat of chapter 8; that is,

both represent the Greek empire which divided into four after
Alexander's death. The only reasonable deduction to draw is
that there are two little horns involved in the symbolic visions
of Daniel. One of them emerges from the third empire, and the
other is to emerge from the fourth. It would seem that the
relationship is that of type (Antiochus IV of the third kingdom)
and antitype (the Antichrist who is to arise from the latter-day
form of the fourth empire). This is the only explanation which
satisfies all the data and which throws light upon 11:40ff.,
where the figure of the historic Antiochus suddenly blends
into the figure of an Antichrist who is yet to come in the end
time." 3/398

In the *International Standard Bible Encyclopedia*, C. M. Cobern
shows how the ram's reference to Persia instead of Greece (and
Alexander) further supports Daniel's genuineness.
Concerning Alexander, he writes: "The most memorable event
of his stay in Egypt was his expedition to the oracle of Jupiter
Ammon (Amen-Ra) where he was declared the son of the god.
To the Egyptians this meant no more than that he was regarded
a lawful monarch, but he pretended to take this declaration as
assigning to him a Divine origin like so many Homeric heroes.
Henceforward there appeared on coins Alexander's head
adorned with the ram's horn of Amen-Ra. This impressed the
eastern imagination so deeply that Mohammed, a thousand
years after, calls him in the Quran *Iskander dhu al-qarnain*,
'Alexander the lord of the two horns.' It is impossible to believe
that the writer of Dnl. could, in the face of the universal
attribution of the two ram's horns to Alexander, represent
Persia, the power he overthrew, as a two-horned ram (Dnl.
8:3,20), unless he had written before the expedition into
Egypt." 72/92

Archer adds to this argument: ". . . the fourth empire of
chapter 2, as corroborated by the other symbolic
representations of chapter 7, clearly pointed forward to the
establishment of the Roman empire, it can only follow that we
are dealing here with genuine predictive prophecy and not a
mere *vaticinium ex eventu*. According to the Maccabean date
theory, Daniel was composed between 168 and 165 B.C.,
whereas the Roman empire did not commence (for the Jews at
least) until 63 B.C., when Pompey the Great took over that part
of the Near East which included Palestine. To be sure,
Hannibal had already been defeated by Scipio at Zama in 202
B.C., and Antiochus III had been crushed at Magnesia in 190,
but the Romans had still not advanced beyond the limits of
Europe by 165, except to establish a vassal kingdom in Asia
Minor and a protectorate over Egypt.

"This one circumstance alone, then, that Daniel predicts the Roman empire, is sufficient to overthrow the entire Maccabean date hypothesis (which of course was an attempt to explain away the supernatural element of prediction and fulfillment). As we shall presently see, there are other remarkable predictions in this book which mark it as of divine inspiration and not a mere historical novel written in the time of the Maccabees." 3/399

In other words, even if Daniel had been written around 165 B.C., the writer could not have foreseen the power and extent of Roman influence (assuming the fourth kingdom describes Rome, which careful analysis dictates) unless the visions were of a supernatural source.

If this is true, then the argument against genuine predictive prophecy is abated. If the prophecies of Rome are genuine, then all the predictive and supernatural elements in Daniel must be granted viable. The writings, therefore, have an integrity that forces back their composition to the sixth century B.C., the time the book itself claims to have been written by Daniel.

Archer gives a final conclusion: "But certainly, as things stood in 165 B.C., no human being could have predicted with any assurance that the Hellenic monarchies of the Near East would be engulfed by the new power which had arisen in the West. No man then living could have foreseen that this Italian republic would have exerted a sway more ruthless and widespread than any empire that had ever preceded it." 3/399

3C. ADMITTED BY CRITICS

S.R. Driver, a radical critic, admits that Daniel made accurate predictions. Driver cites Dillman, a German scholar, as saying: ". . . the course of events in the immediate future, the fall of the tyrant after 3½ years, and the triumph of the saints of God, is defined beforehand by the author as certainly as by any prophet of the olden time. Upon this account chiefly he has obtained recognition in the Jewish Church, if not as a prophet, at least as a man inspired of God. It is, moreover, exactly in virtue of this true perception of the present and of the immediate future, that his book is distinguished, very much to its advantage, from the later Jewish Apocalypses." 12/481

Driver continues: "He does not write *after* the persecutions are ended (in which case his prophecies would be pointless), but *at their beginning*, when his message of encouragement would have a value for the godly Jews in the season of their trial. He thus utters genuine predictions. . . ." 12/478

3B.   The Manuscript Evidence — Qumran

B. K. Waltke states the issue: "The discovery of manuscripts of Daniel at Qumran dating from the Maccabean period renders it highly improbable that the book was composed during the time of the Maccabees." 74/321

1C.   THE DATE OF THE QUMRAN MANUSCRIPT

Soon after the results began to be published on the Dead Sea Scrolls, 17 fragments of Daniel were uncovered, with more to come. Dupont-Sommer in *Aperçus Préliminaires* writes that "The owners of seventeen fragments of Daniel are known, but there are undoubtedly more." 84/17 And presently, one Daniel manuscript cannot be dated later than 120 B.C. on the basis of its paleography. 85/36

2C.   ACCEPTANCE OF EVIDENCE CONCERNING BOOKS OTHER THAN DANIEL

The dating of other Old Testament books during the Maccabean period, books which do not have predictive prophecy or in which predictive prophecy is not a key element, has been largely rejected by contemporary scholars.

W. H. Brownlee, professor of religion at the Claremont Graduate School, concludes that the research of Frank Cross indicates that "one of the Psalms manuscripts from Cave Four attests so-called Maccabean psalms at a period which is roughly contemporary with their supposed composition. If this is true, it would seem that we should abandon the idea of any of the canonical psalms being of Maccabean date, for each song had to win its way in the esteem of the people before it could be included in the sacred compilation of the Psalter. Immediate entree for any of them is highly improbable." 85/29,30

Millar Burrows expands the above reasoning to the date of Ecclesiastes: "The script [of two scrolls of Ecclesiastes found in Cave Four] indicates a date near the middle of the second century B.C. This is not much later than the time at which many scholars have thought the book was originally written. We cannot tell, of course, how old the book was when this particular copy was made, but the probability of its composition in the third century, if not earlier, is somewhat enhanced by finding the manuscript probably not written much after 150 B.C." 82/171

This also holds true for Chronicles. A Maccabean date is almost impossible for Chronicles as a result of a manuscript fragment discovered at Qumran. 83/165

3C. REJECTION OF EVIDENCE CONCERNING DANIEL

Frank Cross, professor at Harvard and authority on the Dead Sea Scrolls, is forced to admit that the Qumran community had the near originals of Daniel even though the Daniel manuscripts at Qumran are dated around 165 B.C., the time the critics claim Daniel was written. Yet, Cross does not say why Daniel had to originate in Qumran. 80/199 ff.

Waltke summarizes: "But critical scholars have refused to draw the same conclusion in the case of Daniel [as they did with many psalms] even though the evidence is identical. For example, in the work cited above by Brownlee he avers the 165 B.C. date in spite of the evidence. His refusal to allow the evidence to lead him to the more probable conclusion that Daniel was composed before the Maccabean era is all the more astonishing because he thinks, along with others, that the late pious forger of Daniel made a mistake in one of his predictions. 'The predicted end of Antiochus in 11:40-45 differs from the stories of his death in I and II Maccabees and hence it presumably represents real prediction on the part of the author of Daniel which was never fulfilled.' But if this be so, it seems incredible that the alleged contemporaries would have held his work in such high regard and refer to him as 'Daniel the prophet,' a title bestowed on him in a *florilegium* found in 4Q." 74/322

4B. Evidence of Other Ancient Writings

1C. BOOK OF EZEKIEL

The Book of Ezekiel gives further evidence that Daniel was a historical figure. In Ezekiel 14:14 and 14:20, Daniel is noted with Noah and Job for his righteousness. Ezekiel 28:3 says, "Behold, you are wiser than Daniel." This representation of Daniel as righteous and wise is in perfect harmony with the Book of Daniel.

The critics claim Ezekiel was referring to a legendary figure of Ugaritic mythology. But would a pious Jew in the Babylonian period use the example of a legendary pagan figure to encourage his people in times of persecution? That certainly is not the pattern of other apocalyptic and prophetic literature. 32/329,330 Hebrew literature is based on historical persons, not mythological characters.

O. T. Allis gives some details about the legendary Daniel whom the critics claim Ezekiel refers to: "One of the first tablets from Ras Shamra to be published (1932) tells the story or myth of a Dn'il (Daniel) who is childless and prays for a son. His prayer is granted. But when his son Aqhat grows up the goddess Anath destroys him because he refused to give her his bow. Daniel recovers his body from the craw of the vulture that has devoured it and buries it. He mourns for Aqhat seven years. Whether Aqhat is finally restored to him or replaced by another son can only be guessed, since the rest of the tablet is mutilated and it is uncertain whether this tablet is part of a series. The title of the poem seems to have been simply, 'Pertaining to Aqhat'; and Ginsberg points out that 'closer study reveals that the text really tells about Daniel only what concerns Aqhat.' " 1/370; 30/149-155

Allis adds: "Yet ever since the tablet was published the claim has been made, sometimes very positively, that it is this Daniel who is referred to by the prophet Ezekiel. This claim is based chiefly on the similarity of the name and on a single brief passage in the poem which reads as follows: 'Straightway Daniel the Rapha-man, Forthwith *Ghazir* the Harnamiyy-man, is upright, sitting before the gate, beneath a mighty tree on the threshing floor, judging the cause of the widow, adjudicating the case of the fatherless.' This is certainly very meager evidence on which to base a theory that Ezekiel is here referring to this legendary figure of Ugaritic lore." 1/370; 30/151

It is difficult to discover a more spurious claim than this attempt by the critics to equate the Daniel of Ezekiel with this pagan figure.

The name Daniel was familiar to the Jewish community. One of King David's 19 sons was named Daniel (I Chronicles 3:1). Ezra 8:2 and Nehemiah 10:6 list Daniel among the names of priests involved in the rebuilding of Jerusalem. Thus Daniel was both a historical and a contemporary name.

The critics think it is remarkable that Ezekiel should refer to a young contemporary along with the ancient Noah and Job. But Ezekiel's ministry did not begin until 592 B.C., about 14 years after Daniel's deportation. Daniel had plenty of time to build his reputation, especially considering the spectacular things he did. 32/329,330

Also, since Ezekiel wrote during the captivity, it would be natural for him to refer to some contemporary godly man to instill hope within the people that God was still at work, even in their captivity.

2C.   FIRST BOOK OF MACCABEES

In the First Book of Maccabees, Mattathias, father of the Maccabean brothers, encourages his sons in the revolt against Antiochus Epiphanes by recalling to them the deeds of their fathers. In I Maccabees 2 he is quoted as saying, "Ananias, Azarias, and Misael, by believing, were saved out of the flame.

Daniel for his innocency was saved from the mouth of lions"
(*cf.* Daniel 3 and 6). Mattathias died in 166 B.C., a year before
the date that critics assign to Daniel. In addition, the context
seems to indicate that Mattathias was referring to an event far
in the past. If Mattathias said this, then the late date theory
cannot be maintained. The critics claim the author of the book
erroneously attributed this saying to him. But if this is the case,
then the author must have thought that Mattathias knew about
the Book of Daniel. The context of the reference seems to
indicate that the author considered Daniel canonical, and in
that case, it must have preceded the Maccabees by many years.

Another point to be made is that the author of I Maccabees
shows familiarity with the Septuagint version of Daniel. The
Book of Daniel had to exist long before Antiochus Epiphanes to
allow sufficient time for its translation into Greek. 43/98-100

An argument which is particularly poignant concerns the
Septuagint translation of some specific Aramaic words used to
designate government officials. Both the translators of the
Septuagint and Theodotian have trouble translating these
technical words in Daniel 3:2. (*E.g.*, "counselor" is translated
"grandees"; "treasurers" is translated "administrators,
governors"; "magistrates" or "judges" is translated "those in
authority.") But if Daniel is dated in the Maccabean period, the
translators would not have had such problems so few years
after Daniel was supposedly composed. The Jews during this
time retained the ability to speak both Aramaic and Greek. The
implications of this argument form a strong case against a
second century date. 3/388

3C.   BOOK OF BARUCH

Wilson evaluates the Book of Baruch as follows: "Chapters i and
ii of the apocryphal Book Baruch are assigned by some scholars
to the fourth century before Christ. If this date be correct, then
the writer of that book would seem to have known the Book of
Daniel, which must in that case have been in existence long
before the Maccabees. In i, ii of Baruch the author bids men
pray for Nabuchodonosor, King of Babylon and for Balthasar
his son. How did he learn of Belshazzar? He could have learned
it from the Book of Daniel, and undoubtedly he did. There is no
other book, of which we now know, containing Belshazzar's
name." 43/96,97

5B.   Other Factors

1C.   TESTIMONY OF CHRIST

Christ refers to "the abomination of desolation which was
spoken of through Daniel the prophet" (Matthew 24:15; *cf.*

Daniel 9:27; 11:31; 12:11). Christ obviously must have regarded Daniel to be historical and the author of these prophecies to use this distinctive phrase. According to Christ's testimony in the Olivet Discourse, the fulfillment of this sign was still in the future (after A.D. 30); it was not fulfilled by Antiochus Epiphanes in 168-165 B.C. as the critics suggest. 3/386

Christ's statement in Matthew 24:15 is even more significant since Daniel's three references to the "abomination of desolation" come from sections that all of the liberal critics believe to be of Maccabean origin. 50/351

Raven concludes: "The statement is so explicit that there are only two alternatives to those who deny that Daniel wrote the book — either that Christ spoke ignorantly or that he accommodates himself to the erroneous opinion of his day." 32/329

Cartledge attempts to explain away Christ's statements: "Jesus may have known that the book was written by someone else and still have spoken of it in a popular way. Or the 'emptying' of which Paul spoke may have kept the incarnate Jesus from having complete knowledge about certain non-essential things: He may simply have used the current tradition." 7/221

In answer to Cartledge, if Jesus knew the book was written by someone else, then He was guilty of deception. He should have said nothing or corrected the mistake. On the other hand, if Jesus spoke from ignorance, He Himself was deceived. Cartledge elsewhere says Christ admitted He did not know the time of His own coming, showing He lacked knowledge in some areas. But there is no evidence in the New Testament record that Jesus had less than complete knowledge concerning any fact which He affirmed. He always spoke with the utmost degree of authority, which could be based only on the certainty that no gaps existed in His knowledge.

As for the time of His return, Jesus did not say that He didn't know the general time, but rather that neither He nor the angels nor anyone but God the Father knew the exact day and hour (Matthew 24:36). This is the only time that Jesus confessed a lack of knowledge. In everything else He talked about He revealed the most comprehensive knowledge imaginable.

One distinction of Christ's teaching is that He never simply used tradition — He corrected tradition, pointing out its errors (Matthew 5:27-30, 43-48; 15:1-20; Mark 7:1-23).

Keil states: "If the book of Daniel were thus a production of a Maccabean Jew, who would bring 'certain wholesome truths' which he thought he possessed before his contemporaries as prophecies of a divinely enlightened seer of the time of the exile, then it contains neither prophecy given by God, nor in general wholesome divine truth, but mere human invention, which because it was clothed with falsehood could not have its origin in the truth. Such a production Christ, the eternal personal Truth, never could have regarded as the prophecy of Daniel the prophet, and commended to the observation of His disciples, as He has done (Matthew xxiv. 15, cf. Mark xiii. 14)." 23/57

2C. ALEXANDER THE GREAT

In his *Antiquities of the Jews,* Josephus relates a story which, if accurate, proves the Book of Daniel existed during the time of Alexander the Great (*c.* 330 B.C.). Alexander, angry with the Jews who refused to give him their allegiance, was going to Jerusalem to punish them and make them an example. When he arrived, however, a procession of priests, which he had foreseen in a dream, met him. In this dream, God had promised him victory, and for this reason he spared the Jews. Josephus adds that the priests showed Alexander the prophecies in Daniel concerning a Greek conquering the Persian empire. This pleased Alexander, and he treated the Jews with kindness.

Circumstances in history support Josephus' story. Alexander marched through that area on his way to Egypt, capturing every city as he went. Without question, he treated the Jews kindly. History also shows that Alexander was a romantic and much given to oracles, omens and the like. 43/101,102

In the International Standard Bible Encyclopedia, C. M. Cobern states: ". . . still it contains no element of improbability that the pupil of Aristotle, in the pursuit of knowledge, might, during the prosecution of the siege of Gaza, with a small company press into the hill country of Judaea, at once to secure the submission of Jerusalem which occupied a threatening position in regard to his communications, and to see something of that mysterious nation who worshipped one God and had no idols." 72/92

3C. VISIT OF THE MAGI

The wise men's visit to the baby Jesus from the East can be understood if they were familiar in some way (such as tradition) with Daniel's prophecy of the 70 weeks (chapter 9). The Roman historians, Tacitus and Suetonius, refer to a widespread anticipation in the East of a great leader arising in Judea at about this time in history. If Daniel was known in the East as a man of extraordinary wisdom who wrote in Babylon, then the wise men might very well have been familiar with his prophecy and looking for its fulfillment. 43/106,107

chapter 3
Attacks on Daniel as a Historian

3A. HISTORICAL ARGUMENTS

The first two critical arguments presented concern factors external to Daniel; the remaining historical arguments concern points of contention within the book.

1B. Position in the Jewish Canon

1C. INTRODUCTION

The Old Testament books are divided into three divisions — the Law, the Prophets and the Writings (also called the Psalms, or the Holy Writings, *i.e.*, the *Hagiographa*).

In the Massoretic Hebrew Bible the books in each division are as follows:

The Law (Torah) — Genesis, Exodus, Leviticus, Numbers, Deuteronomy.

The Prophets (Nebiim) — Joshua, Judges, I and II Samuel, I and II Kings, Isaiah, Jeremiah, Ezekiel and the 12 Minor Prophets.

The Writings (Kethubim) — Psalms, Proverbs, Job, Song of Solomon, Ruth, Lamentations, Ecclesiastes, Esther, Daniel, Ezra, Nehemiah, I and II Chronicles. 43/82

2C. DEDUCTIONS OF THE RADICAL CRITICS

Daniel, though a prophetic book, is not found in the second division of the Jewish canon, the Prophets, but in the third division. The critics claim this supports their view that Daniel was written in the second century B.C.

Dr. Driver states: ". . . the division known as the 'Prophets' was doubtless formed prior to the Hagiographa; and had the Book of Daniel existed at the time, it is reasonable to suppose that it would have ranked as the work of a prophet, and have been included among the former." 12/467

According to E. L. Curtis: "The place of the Book of Daniel among the Hagiographa favors also its late composition. If it had been written during the Exile, notwithstanding its apocalyptic character, it naturally would have been placed among the Prophets." 52/554 ff.; 45/11

Cornill contends: "Among objective reasons of the utmost weight, which render the view of its non-genuineness necessary, *the position of the book in the Hebrew Canon, where it is inserted, not among the prophets, but in the third division of the canon, the so-called Hagiographa*. If it were the work of a prophet of the time of Cyrus, no reason would be evident why there should be withheld from it a designation which was not denied to a Haggai, Zechariah, and Malachi — nay, even to a Jonah." 55/384-386; 45/11

A. A. Bevan (*A Short Commentary on the Book of Daniel*, p. 11) states this opinion: "In the Hebrew Scriptures 'Daniel has never occupied a place among the prophetical Books, but is included in the third collection of sacred writings, called the Kethubim or Hagiographa. Of the history of the Jewish Canon very little is known with certainty, but there is every reason to believe that the collection of Prophetical Books, from which lessons were read in the Synagogue, was definitely closed sometime before the Hagiographa, of which the greater part had no place in the public services. That the collection of Prophetical Books cannot have been completed till sometime after the Exile, is obvious, and on the supposition that Daniel was then known to the Jews, the exclusion of this book is wholly inexplicable.' " 45/10

Prince, in his *Commentary on Daniel* (pp. 15, 16), explains the implications of this opinion: "The position of the book among the Hagiographa instead of among the Prophetical works would seem to indicate that it must have been introduced after the closing of the Prophetical Canon. . . . The natural explanation regarding the position of the Book of Daniel is that the work could not have been in existence at the time of the completion of the second part of the Canon, as otherwise, the collectors of the prophetical writings, who in their care did not neglect even the parable of Jonah, would hardly have ignored the record of such a great prophet as Daniel is represented to be." 45/11

3C. EVALUATING CRITICAL CONTENTIONS

    1D.   Assumption: The prophetic section of the canon was closed before the *Hagiographa* section was closed.

    2D.   Assumption: The time of a book's writing determined:

         1.   When it was accepted into the canon.

         2.   Where it was placed in the canon.

3D. Deduction: The position of a book in the canon dictates when it was written.

4D. Fact: Daniel is obviously a prophetic writing.

5D. Deductive assumption: If Daniel had been known before the prophetic section was closed, it would have been included.

6D. Deduction: Since Daniel was not included in the prophetic section, it was not known at the time the section was closed.

7D. Deduction: Since Daniel was not known at that time, it had not been written.

4C. ANSWERS

We must examine the assumptions and deductive assumption, which form the basis of the critics' deductions.

1D. Formation of the Canon

Dr. Charles H. Wright *(Daniel and His Prophecies,* p. 50) observes: "There is nothing worthy to be regarded as real 'evidence' concerning the settlement of the so-called Canon of the Old Testament Scriptures. No one can prove when or by what authority the books of the Old Testament were arranged into three distinct divisions. It is vain to speak of three distinct canons, and to assign a date for the closing up of each division. These attempts rest on unhistorical conjectures." 4/276

From a look at the three divisions of the Old Testament, we observe the following:

1. Labels of the three divisions do not form exclusive categories.

2. The prophetic and writings sections include both historical and prophetic books.

3. Some of the third division (Job, Ruth, Proverbs, Song of Solomon and many of the Psalms) were written before certain books in the second division (Kings and Isaiah to Malachi).

According to H. S. Miller, the theory that best fits the evidence states that "the real ground of division is the official position, or status, of the writers. The books of the first section were written by Moses, the great lawgiver and founder of the Old Testament economy; those of the second by men who had the prophetic office as well as the prophetic gift; those of the third by men who had the prophetic gift but not the prophetic office, inspired men but not official prophets." 56/94

This explains why Joshua, Judges, Samuel and Kings are in the second division and Chronicles is not; why historical writings are in both divisions; and why Daniel and Ezekiel, though the authors were contemporaries, are in separate divisions.

The radical critics maintain that the divisions in the canon are the product of three mutually exclusive periods of collection and canonization. This view fails to consider that several books in the third division are older than some of the books in the second division.

Erwin Jenkins states: "But this three stage theory fails to agree with the statement of Josephus who said that there was no other Scripture added after 424 B.C., the death of Artaxerxes." 21/23

If Malachi (last book in the Prophets) was the last inspired book, as Jewish tradition claims, then the second division could not have been closed before the third division. The critics' theory also fails to explain why the third division is called "Other Writings," or why the third division was started at all and kept separate from the second division. 32/39

As for the evidence, Driver admits that "little definite is known respecting the formation of the Canon." 12/447; 45/10

Bevan also admits that "of the history of the Jewish Canon very little is known." 45/10

R. D. Wilson concludes: "It will be observed that, while admitting that little is known, the critics indulge in such phrases and words as 'doubtless,' 'reasonable to suppose,' 'seem to indicate,' 'every reason to believe,' 'supposition,' 'not easy to reconcile,' 'inexplicable,' 'natural explanation,' and so forth. All of these words and phrases are admissions on the part of the critics that their theory with regard to the Book of Daniel is not convincingly supported by the evidence, even themselves being witnesses." 45/13

2D.   Daniel Not Officially a Prophet

Daniel does not introduce his book with his name, but presents himself as one of the Jewish exiles in the court of Babylon. He had no official position among the Jewish people, as far as we know, and even in exile, he was neither a prophet nor a religious reformer. 32/318

The radical critic S. R. Driver admits that Daniel was not a prophet: "The author, it may be noticed, does not claim to speak with the special authority of the 'prophet'; he never uses the prophetical asseverations, 'Thus saith Jehovah,' 'Saith Jehovah.' " 12/481

Raven writes: "Although Daniel possessed the spirit of prophecy to a marked degree, his office and his work were altogether exceptional. He was not living among the exiles like Ezekiel but [lived] at the court of Babylon, and he had to do with heathen kings rather than with the people of Israel. In the New Testament, like David, (Acts 2:29-30) he is called a prophet because of his predictions." 32/41,42

R. K. Harrison, professor of Old Testament at Wycliffe College, asserts: "The fact is that critical scholars have made out an extremely poor case for a Maccabean dating (for example, the summary by S. B. Frost, *IDB*, I, p. 765), and the weaknesses of their position have become even more evident since the discovery of the Qumran manuscripts. Although an almost desperate appeal has been made to the fact that Daniel occurs in the third section of the Hebrew canon rather than among the prophets in the second section as an indication of late date, this circumstance merely testifies that Daniel was not regarded as having occupied the prophetic office as such. He was not a prophet in the classic sense associated with Amos, Isaiah, Jeremiah, and others of the literary coterie for the simple reason that he did not function as a spiritual mediator between God and a theocratic community, despite the fact that he was endowed with certain conspicuous prophetic gifts. . . ." 19/1123

Harrison concludes: "Like Joseph of old, he was a Hebrew statesman in a heathen court, and not a 'writing prophet' or spiritual mediator in the commonly understood sense." 19/1123

3D. Daniel Originally in Prophetic Section?

The Book of Daniel would not be out of place in the prophetic section. Joshua, Judges and Kings are included in the Prophets, and the translators of the Septuagint version of the Jewish Scriptures placed Daniel there also. 43/84

As Charles Boutflower, vicar of Terling, Essex, says: ". . . *the present position of the Book in the Hebrew Canon is not its original position.* We have it on the authority of the Jewish priest-historian Josephus — one who in such a matter could make no mistake — that at the close of the first century A.D. the Canon of the Old Testament books was differently arranged from that at present accepted among the Jews; and it is also evident from the writings of the Early Fathers that a change must have been made in the arrangement of the Jewish Canon between the middle of the third and the end of the fourth century A.D." 4/276,277

Josephus in *Contra Apionem* 1:8 writes: "We have but twenty-two [books] containing the history of all time, books that are justly believed in; and of these, five are the books of Moses, which comprise the laws and earliest traditions from the creation of mankind down to his death. From the death of Moses to the reign of Artaxerxes, King of Persia, the successor of Xerxes, the prophets who succeeded Moses wrote the history of the events that occurred in their own time, in thirteen books. The remaining four documents comprise hymns to God and practical precepts to men."

Daniel was included in these 13 books. The conclusion is that Chronicles, Esther, Ezra, Nehemiah, Daniel and Song of Solomon were not added to the third division (*Kethubim*) of the Hebrew canon until after the first century A.D.

Professor Wilson states: "All the direct evidence, then, that precedes the year 200 A.D., supports the view that Daniel was in the earliest times among the Prophets. Further, this conclusion is supported by all the direct evidence outside the Talmud, which is later than A.D. 200. Thus Origen, at A.D. 250, and Jerome, at A.D. 400, both of whom were taught by Jewish Rabbis and claim to have gained their information from Jewish sources, put Daniel among the Prophets and separate the strictly prophetical books from those which are more properly called historical. And, lastly, all the Greek uncials and the Greek and Latin fathers, unite in placing Daniel among the Prophets and in separating the Prophets from the Historical Books." 45/49

4D. Why Accepted into the Canon?

Strong evidence for Daniel's genuineness is its acceptance into the canon. Jewish religious authorities accepted the book because they considered it authentic, genuine and true. Tobit, Judith, Enoch, Jubilees, The Testament of the Twelve Patriarchs and other apocryphal and pseudepigraphical writings were rejected from the canon because the Jews considered them secondary, questionable or heretical. 44/277

A. T. Pierson (*Many Infallible Proofs*) indicates that the Jews would have included Daniel in the canon only after careful scrutiny. Many of the apocryphal books, though pure in tone and style, were rejected. The crucial test was a book's inspired character; the Jews must have believed in the holy inspiration of Daniel. If Daniel had appeared after the prophecies were fulfilled, it would have been rejected. But, if the book existed before the events, it proved its inspiration. 28/51,52

The greatest proof against the critics' theory that Daniel was written during the reign of Antiochus Epiphanes is found in Daniel 11:40-45. Driver dates Daniel around 168 B.C. DeWette-Schroder dates it between 167 and 164 B.C. Cornill dates it between late December 165 and June 164, the greatest probability being January 164. These critics also claim the Egyptian campaign mentioned in Daniel 11:40-45 never happened. This means that the Jews who lived during this time, who must have known all about Epiphanes and his campaigns, accepted this book shortly after it was written as the genuine work of a great prophet of foregone years, even though it speaks of a whirlwind conquest of Egypt which never occurred. Do the critics believe the people of that day to be so credulous? 45/265,266

God had told the people (Deuteronomy 18:20-22) they were to reject and kill any man claiming to be a prophet whose predictions failed to come true. According to the critics, the events foretold in Daniel 11:40-45 did not occur — the author predicted this end to Antiochus Epiphanes' reign, but guessed wrongly. Why then did the Jews accept the book into the canon when it violated God's expressed criteria? Obviously, they believed that Daniel was genuine and that its authority had been established through the fulfillment of many prophecies made in the sixth century B.C. 3/385,386

R. D. Wilson clarifies the issue: "Now, the radical critics, without any direct evidence to support them, profess to believe that, into the midst of these sacred writings for which men readily died, a forged document of unknown authorship and (according to the critics) full of easily detected errors and of doctrines unrecognized in the Law and the other books of the Prophets was quietly admitted as a genuine and authentic writing of a prophet hitherto unknown to history. They would have us believe that this fictitious volume became immediately the model of a vast amount of similar literature and they admit that in the New Testament its influence is apparent almost everywhere and that 'no writing of the Old Testament had so great a share in the development of Christianity.' They admit, also, that in early times its canonicity and truthfulness were never seriously disputed by Jews or Christians. Truly, the credulity of these critics is pitiable in its eccentricities! They cannot believe in miracles and predictive prophecy which involve nothing but a simple faith in a wise and mighty and merciful God intervening in behalf of his people for his own glory and their salvation; but they can believe that a lot of obstreperous and cantankerous Jews who through all their history from Jacob and Esau down to the present time have disagreed and quarrelled about almost everything, or nothing, could have accepted, unanimously and without a murmur, in an age when they were enlightened by the brilliant light of Plato's philosophy, and Aristotle's logic, and the criticism of the schools of Alexandria, a forged and fictitious document, untrue to the well remembered facts of their own experience and to the easily ascertained facts concerning their own past history and the history of the Babylonians, Medes, Persians, and Greeks of whom the author writes. Such a psychological improbability, devoid of any direct evidence in its support, let the critic believe if he can. Your unsophisticated servant prefers his belief in predictive prophecy to any such quixotic and sciolistic attempts to belittle and besmirch a book simply because we cannot understand the why and the how of all the extraordinary deeds and doctrines that are recorded there." 45/268,269

Sir Robert Anderson, the English scholar, states why Daniel cannot be a fraud: "The Sanhedrin of the second century B.C. was composed of men of the type of John Hyrcanus; men famed for their piety and learning; men who were heirs of all the proud traditions of the Jewish faith, and themselves the sons of successors of the heroes of the nobel Maccabean revolt. And yet we are asked to believe that these men, with their extremely strict views of inspiration and their intense reverence for their sacred writings . . . used their authority to smuggle into the sacred canon a book which, *ex hypothesi*, was a forgery, a literary fraud, a religious novel of recent date." 75/104,105

5C.　SUMMARY

We have shown that:

1. Not enough is known about the canon's formation to prove it was formed in three stages.

2. The evidence indicates that a book's position in the Massoretic canon was based on the author's official status, not on date of writing.

3. Daniel was not officially a prophet; therefore, his book evidently was placed by the Massoretes in the third division (the *Hagiographa*) rather than in the second (the Prophets).

4. Evidently, Daniel originally was included in the second division before being moved to the third in the later period.

2B.　Not Mentioned by Jesus Ben Sirach

1C.　THE PROBLEM

Jesus ben Sirach wrote Ecclesiasticus between 200 and 170 B.C. At the end of the book, he recapitulates Israel's history, mentioning some of the men God has used to lead Israel. Daniel is not included among these. Ben Sirach also states, "Neither was there a man born like unto Joseph" (Ecclesiasticus 49:15).

2C. THE CRITICS' CONTENTIONS

Prince (*Commentary on Daniel*, p. 16 ff.) expresses this opinion: "The silence of Jesus Sirach (Ecclesiasticus) concerning Daniel seems to show that the prophet was unknown to that late writer who, in his list of celebrated men (chap. xlix), makes no mention of Daniel, but passes from Jeremiah to Ezekiel and then to the twelve Minor Prophets and Zerubbabel. If Daniel had been known to Jesus Sirach, we would certainly expect to find his name in this list, probably between Jeremiah and Ezekiel. Again, the only explanation seems to be that the Book of Daniel was not known to Sirach who lived and wrote between 200 and 180 B.C. Had so celebrated a person as Daniel been known, he could hardly have escaped mention in such a complete list of Israel's leading spirits." 45/77,78

Driver notes Ecclesiasticus 49:15, stating that "no man was born upon earth like unto Joseph, whereas the narratives respecting Daniel represent him much like unto Joseph in regard to both the high distinctions he attained and the faculties he displayed; and further, the very wording of the narratives in the first part of Daniel is modelled after that of the narratives in Genesis concerning Joseph." 8/17,64

3C. EVALUATING CRITICAL CONTENTIONS

1D. Contention: Daniel's absence from the list of Israel's notable leaders in Ecclesiasticus proves that Daniel was unknown to ben Sirach.

2D. Claim: The narrative in the first part of Daniel is modeled after the narratives in Genesis concerning Joseph.

3D. Claim: Daniel is similar to Joseph in faculties displayed and distinctions attained.

4D. Inference: If ben Sirach, who meritoriously mentions Joseph, had known of Daniel, he surely would have given him equal recognition.

5D. Deduction: Since ben Sirach states that no man like Joseph had ever been born, he must have known nothing of Daniel.

6D. Deduction: Since ben Sirach, an eminent Jewish writer, had no knowledge of Daniel, the Book of Daniel must not yet have been written.

7D. Deduction: Daniel must not have existed in Jewish history.

4C.   ANSWERS

   1D.   Credibility of Ecclesiasticus

      Ecclesiasticus appears to have been written to morally
      inspire the Jewish people. The first 43 chapters contain moral
      teachings and proverbs. The following section praises the
      famous men and heroes of Jewish history. There is no
      particular reason or occasion for ben Sirach to mention
      Daniel (or Ezra, either), important though he was to Hebrew
      history.

      J. D. Wilson, professor of history at the theological seminary
      of the Reformed Episcopal Church, makes the following
      observation: "But, on the other hand, the position of
      Ecclesiasticus among the uncanonical Jewish books weighs
      strongly against the Maccabean theory. Ecclesiasticus is a
      book of moral teaching. It was highly esteemed in the early
      Christian Church; was read in the public assemblies, is
      quoted with approval by Clement of Alexandria, Dionysius,
      Tertullian, Cyprian, Augustine and others. It presents the
      dominant type of Jewish thought at the time that the Canon
      was taking a fixed form. Its conception of God is Mosaic,
      while legalism is fastening itself more and more in the
      principles and practice of godly men. In short, it presents
      what in the opinion of the Jewish doctors of that day was true
      religion. In moral and religious teaching it was superior to
      several canonical books of the Old Testament and gives the
      finest expression of Palestinian theology of the two or three
      centuries following Nehemiah that we possess. Why then
      was it not included in the Jewish Canon?" 43/77,78

      There is no arbitrary reason why a book composed during
      the intertestamental period could not have qualified for a
      place in the canon, unless it failed to pass the canonical
      criteria. Although Ecclesiasticus has a fine moral quality in
      the section devoted to moral teachings, the author displays a
      magnified self-opinion that readily disqualifies the book
      from having the authority of Scripture.

   2D.   Josephus Chose Not to Include Daniel

      Daniel must have been well known to the Jews of this time
      because he is mentioned in the Book of Ezekiel (14:14-20;
      28:3). (See chapter 2 of this book, 4B, Book of Ezekiel.) Since
      ben Sirach mentions Ezekiel and refers to his visions
      (Ecclesiasticus 49:8), he was familiar with Ezekiel's book and
      must have known of Daniel.

      R. K. Harrison remarks: ". . . that there are allusions to
      Daniel and his book in Maccabees (1 Macc. 2:59ff.), Baruch

(1:15-3:3), and the *Sibylline Oracles* (III, 397ff.), all of which are at least second-century B.C. compositions, and these works attest to the familiarity of the Daniel tradition at that time." 19/1124

In chapters 45-50 of Ecclesiasticus ben Sirach lists the following men, in this order: Enoch, Noah, Abraham, Isaac, Jacob, Moses, Aaron, Phinehas, David, Joshua, Caleb, Samuel, Nathan, Solomon, Elijah, Elisha, Hezekiah, Isaiah, Josiah, Jeremiah, Ezekiel, Zerubbabel, Joshua (son of Josedee), Nehemiah, Joseph, Shem, Seth, Adam, Simon (son of Onias) and Enoch. Such prominent men of the Bible as Mordecai, Ezra and Job are omitted. Ben Sirach clearly did not intend to include everyone worthy of note. The omission of a particular individual does not prove anything. 43/74-76

Raven says that ben Sirach's omission of Ezra is more remarkable than the omission of Daniel, but no one has used this as evidence to deny the existence of Ezra or his book. 32/319

R. K. Harrison states: "A proper assessment of the evidence provided by Ecclesiasticus should include recognition of the possibility that Ben Sira deliberately excluded Daniel from his list of notables for unknown reasons, as he did also with Job and all the Judges except Samuel, as well as Kings Asa and Jehoshaphat, Mordecai, and even Ezra himself. Ecclesiasticus is clearly limited in its usefulness as a ground of appeal for establishing the historicity of certain well-known Hebrew personages, if, indeed, it should ever be employed at all in this manner." 19/1123

R. D. Wilson comments: ". . . there is good reason for supposing that Ben Sira intentionally omitted all references to Daniel, or his book. For the works of Ben Sira show that he was a man of pronounced prejudices and opinions. His views might be characterised as Sadducean and nationalistic. When he gives an account of the great men of his nation, he selects for his encomiums those who had most distinguished themselves according to his ideas of what constituted greatness. We, doubtless, would have added some names that he has omitted from his list. We might have omitted some that he has selected. We certainly would have given more space to the praise of some than he has given, and less to the praise of others. But after all has been said, we will have to admit that there must be granted to him the right and the liberty to praise as he pleases the men whom he wishes to praise. That he has passed by some whom we most highly esteem does not show that he was not aware of their existence. It simply shows that he had reasons of his own, that seemed satisfactory to him, for rejecting them from his list of worthies." 45/76,77

Concerning ben Sirach's qualifications for what made a man famous, Wilson notes: "It is a remarkable fact that he does not pay any regard to the great men who had exercised their functions outside the bounds of the land of Israel, such as Jonah at Nineveh, Daniel in Babylon, and Mordecai in Persia. In speaking of Abraham, he does not refer to his coming out of Ur of the Chaldees, nor to his visit to Egypt. In speaking of Jacob, Joseph, and Aaron, he says nothing of the land of Egypt; nor does he intimate that Moses had ever been in Egypt, saying simply of the wonderful deeds done by him there, that 'God gave him might in terrible wonders,' and that 'through the word of his mouth he caused signs to happen quickly, and caused him to be strong before the king.' Of all the foreign kings mentioned in the Old Testament, he refers to but two — once to Pharaoh and once to Sennacherib. As far as Daniel is concerned, therefore, and the foreign kings among whom he laboured, it is entirely in harmony with the plan of the work of Ben Sira, that no one of them should be noticed." 44/54,55

Notice also that all of the men in ben Sirach's list, from Moses onward, made some direct contribution to the Jewish nation. Daniel's activities, however, had little direct effect on Israel. 45/87

In the moral teachings of Ecclesiasticus, ben Sirach is silent about doctrinal themes that are important in Daniel: prayer and fasting, angels, judgment, the resurrection and immortality. Perhaps ben Sirach disliked the emphasis in Daniel or thought it an insignificant work. The factors that led ben Sirach not to mention Daniel are not at all clear.

3D.   Daniel Not Like Joseph

The critics also point to ben Sirach's statement that Joseph was unique. Since Daniel's career appears similar to Joseph's, the critics claim ben Sirach must not have known about Daniel.

Daniel was like Joseph in some ways, and Mordecai was like him in other ways. Neither gains recognition from ben Sirach. But, unlike Mordecai and Joseph, Daniel was not instrumental in rescuing the Jewish people from a gravely dangerous situation. Daniel's accomplishments were not what ben Sirach deemed significant.

What ben Sirach says about Joseph is interesting, but his failure to mention him in his main discourse is more significant. The three-line reference to Joseph follows ben Sirach's list of important historical figures.

In addition, ben Sirach's statements about Joseph tend to lose their impact because of the exaggerated superlatives and elaborate, fantastic metaphors he uses to praise the historical figures who have gained his favor.

5C. SUMMARY

We have shown that ben Sirach omitted many important figures of Jewish history, not only Daniel. That they were not included was simply a choice of the author. Also, the way ben Sirach refers to Joseph is a product of his exaggerated writing style and personal opinions rather than a conclusion based on facts.

3B. The Date of Nebuchadnezzar's Siege of Jerusalem

This is the beginning of the critics' attempt to discredit Daniel's historical reliability.

1C. INTRODUCTION

1D. The Text

Daniel 1:1-3 states: "In the third year of the reign of Jehoiakim king of Judah, Nebuchadnezzar king of Babylon came to Jerusalem and besieged it. And the Lord gave Jehoiakim king of Judah into his hand, along with some of the vessels of the house of God; and he brought them to the land of Shinar, to the house of his god, and he brought the vessels into the treasury of his god. Then the king ordered Ashpenaz, the chief of his officials, to bring in some of the sons of Israel, including some of the royal family and of the nobles."

2D. Problems with These Verses

II Kings mentions nothing about this event, and Jeremiah implies that by the fourth year of Jehoiakim, the Babylonians had not yet invaded Judah. 12/468

Also, the Babylonian Chronicle makes no reference to action by Nebuchadnezzar in Judah during the third year of Jehoiakim or to a siege of Jerusalem. 47/16

According to Jeremiah 46:2, the battle that supposedly opened the way for a Babylonian invasion of Judah did not occur until the fourth year of Jehoiakim's reign, whereas Daniel 1:1 says Nebuchadnezzar besieged Jerusalem in the third year of Jehoiakim's reign.

2C. REPRESENTATIVE CONTENTIONS OF THE RADICAL CRITICS

Driver concludes: "That Nebuchadnezzar besieged Jerusalem, and carried away some of the sacred vessels in 'the third year of

Jehoiakim' (Dan. 1, 1f.), though it cannot, strictly speaking, be disproved, is highly improbable. . . ." 12/468

Professor Cornill says: "Daniel's fixing the carrying away into captivity in the third year of Jehoiakim (Dan. i, I) contradicts all contemporaneous accounts and can only be explained as due to a combination of 2 Chron. xxxvi, 6,7, with an erroneous interpretation of 2 Kings xxiv, 1." 55/384

Professor Bevan (*A Short Commentary on the Book of Daniel*, p. 16) expresses this belief: "It was not till after the defeat of the Egyptian army at Carchemish on the Euphrates in the fourth year of Jehoiakim (Jer. xlvi, 2) that there could be any question of Nebuchadnezzar's invading Palestine, where for some years the Egyptians had enjoyed undisputed supremacy." 44/63

3C. EVALUATING CRITICAL CONTENTIONS

   1D. Interpretations

      1E. Nebuchadnezzar besieged Jerusalem in the third year of Jehoiakim.

      2E. Nebuchadnezzar defeated Jerusalem in the third year of Jehoiakim.

      3E. Nebuchadnezzar took some of the temple's sacred vessels and some of the sons of Israel to Shinar in the third year of Jehoiakim.

   2D. Historical contention: No contemporary account mentions that Nebuchadnezzar took the temple vessels and the sons of Israel to Shinar in the third year of Jehoiakim.

   3D. Deductive contention: The writer of Daniel must have misinterpreted these events as described in II Chronicles 36:6,7 and II Kings 24:1. (This deduction is based on the belief that Daniel had to rely on those accounts for his knowledge of the events, since he wrote his account in the second century B.C.)

   4D. Historical fact: Egypt had enjoyed undisputed supremacy over Palestine for several years until Nebuchadnezzar defeated the Egyptian army at Carchemish in the fourth year of Jehoiakim, as recorded in Jeremiah 46:2.

   5D. Observation: Jeremiah 46:2 says that Nebuchadnezzar defeated the Egyptians at Carchemish in the fourth year of Jehoiakim, whereas Daniel 1:1 says that Nebuchadnezzar besieged Jerusalem in the third year of Jehoiakim.

   6D. Deductive contention: Nebuchadnezzar could not have

invaded Palestine until he had defeated the Egyptians at Carchemish.

7D.   Conclusion: Daniel is historically inaccurate.

4C.   CONTENT OF DANIEL 1:1-3

1D.   During the third year of Jehoiakim's reign, Nebuchadnezzar besieged Jerusalem.

2D.   The Lord gave Jerusalem and some of the temple vessels to Nebuchadnezzar.

3D.   Nebuchadnezzar took Jehoiakim and the temple vessels to Shinar.

4D.   Nebuchadnezzar ordered some of the exceptional youths of Israel brought to Shinar.

5C.   QUESTIONS IN DISPUTE
When did Nebuchadnezzar:

1.   Arrive at Jerusalem and besiege it?

2.   Defeat Jerusalem?

3.   Carry away captives and sacred vessels?

At this point, the sequence of events concerning Nebuchadnezzar's siege of Jerusalem and capture of certain Jewish youths and temple vessels must be established, because II Kings and II Chronicles record three separate occasions when Nebuchadnezzar carried away persons and articles of the temple.

1D.   II Kings 23:36-24:5; II Chronicles 36:5-8

Jehoiakim gave allegiance to Nebuchadnezzar for three years and then rebelled against him; this resulted in Nebuchadnezzar's siege against Jerusalem. Nebuchadnezzar apparently defeated Jehoiakim's forces, because Jehoiakim was bound in chains and taken to Babylon with some articles from the Jewish temple, thus ending his 11-year reign (597 B.C.). The accounts do not say when the siege of Jerusalem began or how long it lasted.

2D.   II Kings 24:8-16; II Chronicles 36:9,10

Jehoiachin succeeded Jehoiakim and reigned for three months, during which the servants of Nebuchadnezzar besieged Jerusalem. This time they must have completed the capture, because Nebuchadnezzar took Jehoiachin and the royal family, all the important officials, military leaders, skilled workers and the royal and temple treasures to Babylon. This was obviously a complete capitulation. It is possible that the exile of Jehoiakim's family and capture of a few temple vessels demonstrated Judah's partial acquiescence to the Babylonians with the hope that this would appease them. That only three months elapsed before total surrender, however, seems to indicate the siege was maintained throughout. Perhaps Jehoiakim agreed to serve Babylon to save his life.

Concerning the tribute, D. J. Wiseman states: "It would seem that Jehoiakim took part of the temple treasure as a qatre-offering or as *biltu* (tribute) to buy off the Babylonians, much as had Hezekiah in keeping the Assyrians at bay (2 Ki. 18:13-16). Jehoiakim may have been personally required to go to Babylon to take part in the victory celebration as conquered and vassal king (2 Ch. 36:6), as had Menasseh in the days of Esarhaddon (2 Ch. 33:11). The Old Testament is our only record of both these events." 47/18

Daniel implies that Nebuchadnezzar took some temple vessels and hostages as a bribe or show of good faith. Temple treasure had been used as payment for peace by Asa (I Kings 15:18), Jehoash (II Kings 12:18) and Hezekiah (II Kings 18:15,16). If a Jew did write Daniel in the second century B.C., he would not have composed an apparent contradiction to Jeremiah's writings. 19/1112,1113; 9/35; 50/356

It is possible, then, that the surrenders of Jehoiakim and Jehoiachin and the capture first of the temple vessels and then of all the temple treasure represent two stages of the same event which occurred in the eighth year of Nebuchadnezzar's reign (II Kings 24:12). However, the text of II Chronicles 36:10 does not say "few" in the Hebrew, but rather "the vessels of delight of the house of Yahweh," which could include all of the important vessels. Hence there is no demonstrable discrepancy with II Kings 24:13: "all the treasures of the house of Yahweh, and the treasures of the king's house," and "cut in pieces all the vessels of gold in the temple of Yahweh."

3D.   II Kings 24:17-25:21; II Chronicles 36:11-20

Zedekiah, after ruling for a few years, also rebelled against Nebuchadnezzar. In the ninth year of Zedekiah's reign, Nebuchadnezzar again besieged Jerusalem, which fell in the 11th year of Zedekiah's reign (586 B.C.). This time the retribution was more severe. Jerusalem was destroyed, the leading men were killed, and those left alive were taken to Babylon with all remaining articles from the temple. This final destruction occurred in the 19th year of Nebuchadnezzar's reign.

Seen against this framework of events, Daniel 1:1 apparently refers to Nebuchadnezzar's initial siege against Jerusalem in the first year of his reign and the third year of Jehoiakim's reign (605 B.C.). Judah became a vassal-state of Babylon. Further research shows that Daniel used the Babylonian accession year system, but Jeremiah in 46:2 used the non-accession year system. Both come out to 605 B.C. 3/381

Daniel 1:2 refers to the siege against Jerusalem following Jehoiakim's subsequent rebellion in 598. Jehoiakim seems to have *died* three months before the capitulation to Nebuchadnezzar. Jehoiachin was taken, but not Jehoiakim. (*cf.* II Kings 24:6: "He slept with his fathers" before Jehoiachin acceded.)

Daniel 1:2 means that Jehoiakim and his troops were defeated on the field and were turned over to the Chaldean power. It does not mean that he personally was taken off to Babylon into captivity. The events of Daniel 1:3 seem to fit in best with Jerusalem's surrender to Nebuchadnezzar in 597 and the exile of Jehoiachin, the royal family, important officials and skilled workers.

Thus Daniel 1:1-4 is a brief summary of pertinent events leading up to the person and life of Daniel and his position and influence in the royal court of Nebuchadnezzar. This summary is not concerned with all the exact details, such as whether Nebuchadnezzar conducted the siege of Jerusalem in person or through his deputy commanders.

6C. ANSWERS

1D. Jerusalem Was Besieged, Not Captured

Some radical critics argue that Jerusalem was not captured until 597 B.C., several years after Nebuchadnezzar's Carchemish campaign against the Egyptians. B. W. Anderson takes this position: "The book begins with a glaring historical error, for Nebuchadnezzar did not take Jerusalem in the third year of King Jehoiakim (606 B.C.)." 88/540

Daniel never states, however, that Jerusalem was captured in Jehoiakim's third year (605 B.C.). He merely says Nebuchadnezzar besieged Jerusalem.

Berosus (in the fragments of his *Chaldaic History* preserved by Josephus) explains why Jerusalem was not captured at that time: "When his (Nebuc.) father Nabopolassar heard that the satrap whom he had set over Egypt and over the parts of Coelesyria and Phoenicia had revolted from him, he was unable to bear the annoyance any longer, but committing a part of his army to his son Nabuchodonosor, who was then a youth, he sent him against the rebel. Nabuchodonosor encountered him in battle and overcame him, and brought the land again under his dominion. It happened that his father Nabopolassar at this time fell sick and died at the city of Babylon, after he had reigned twenty-one years (Berosus says twenty-nine years). But when Nabuchodonosor not long after heard of the death of his father, he set the affairs of Egypt and of the other countries in order, and committed the prisoners he had taken from the Jews, the Phoenicians, and Syrians, and from the nations belonging to Egypt, to some of his friends, that they might conduct the heavy armed troops with the rest of the baggage to Babylonia, while he himself hastened with a small escort through the desert to Babylon." 22/224,225, 613

C. F. Keil comments on Berosus: "This fragment illustrates in an excellent manner the statements made in the Bible. . . . For Berosus confirms not only the fact, as declared in 2 Kings xxiv. 7, that Pharaoh-Necho in the last year of Nabopolassar, after the battle at Megiddo, had subdued Judah, Phoenicia, and Coelesyria, *i.e.* 'all the land from the river of Egypt unto the river Euphrates,' but he also bears witness to the fact that Nebuchadnezzar, after he had slain Pharaoh-Necho (Jer. xlvi. 2) 'by the river Euphrates in Carchemish,' made Coelesyria, Phoenicia, and Judah tributary to the Chaldean empire, and consequently that he took Jerusalem not before but after the battle at Carchemish, in prosecution of the victory he had obtained over the Egyptians." 23/63-65

It will be helpful at this point to reconstruct what was happening during this time. The Assyrian empire had dominated the Fertile Crescent region from about 885-626 B.C. To the east lay the Median empire; to the west lay Egypt. Babylon, an ancient city-state, was located in the plain of Shinar along with a number of Chaldean city-states. When the Assyrian empire weakened, Nabopolassar, a Chaldean prince, defeated an Assyrian army near Babylon. He then joined forces with Cyaxeres, leader of the Medes, and captured Nineveh, the Assyrian capital. These victories marked the beginning of the Chaldean empire.

Nabopolassar destined Nebuchadnezzar to be his successor and appointed him as his representative to the Chaldean army.

Near the end of Nabopolassar's reign, Pharaoh Necho II of Egypt also took advantage of Assyria's weakness to try to conquer Syria and Palestine. Necho's army was crossing the central plain of the Fertile Crescent in an effort to sieze that

whole area, but at Carchemish in 605 B.C. Necho
encountered another rising force, the Chaldeans under
Nebuchadnezzar. The Egyptians were routed and pursued
all the way back to the borders of Egypt. They did not again
attempt to conquer Syria and Palestine militarily, but tried
continually to stir up a rebellion there against Chaldean rule.

Before the battle at Carchemish, Josiah, king of Judah, had
attempted to lead his forces against Necho, but he was
defeated and killed in the Battle of Megiddo in 609. Necho
then appointed Jehoiakim as king, subservient to Egypt.
Four years after this (Carchemish, 605), Nebuchadnezzar
defeated Necho, and Jehoiakim changed his allegiance to
Nebuchadnezzar. Later on, however, he rebelled and
reverted his allegiance to Egypt (subsequent to Egypt's
stand-off battle with Nebuchadnezzar in 601). 46/29-31,70,71
Nebuchadnezzar then came to Jerusalem to reassert
Chaldean dominance. A shift of allegiance to Egypt occurred
under Jehoiachin and Zedekiah also, each time provoking a
reaction from Nebuchadnezzar that resulted in the other two
occasions when Jewish people and temple vessels were taken
to Babylon.

In the midst of the first Palestinian campaign of 605,
Nebuchadnezzar received word of his father's death and
rushed to Babylon to assume the throne before a usurper
could gain control. (This sudden trip back to Babylon seems
to have happened in September, just two or three months
after the victory at Carchemish in June. In all probability,
Nebuchadnezzar took over Judah in late fall.) He apparently
abandoned the siege against Jerusalem before he captured
the city.

Some radical critics insist that Nebuchadnezzar's first siege
against Jerusalem could not have occurred before the ninth
month of Jehoiakim's fifth year. Keil states that they conclude
from Jeremiah 36:9 that "Nebuchadnezzar's assault upon
Jerusalem was in the ninth month of the fifth year of
Jehoiakim as yet only in prospect, because in that month
Jeremiah prophesied of the Chaldean invasion, and the
extraordinary fast then appointed had as its object the
manifestation of repentance, so that thereby the wrath of
God might be averted." 23/65

Nebuchadnezzar did besiege Jerusalem near the end of
Jehoiakim's reign, several years after his fifth year, but Keil
explains that Jeremiah's prophecy does not preclude a
previous siege against Jerusalem. This prophecy (in chapter
36), announces that total destruction, threatened previously

in Jeremiah 25, still awaits them if the people do not repent.
(Perhaps they thought that Nebuchadnezzar's siege and
their vassalage to him fulfilled that prophecy. Jeremiah let
them know it had not yet been completely fulfilled — worse
things lay ahead.)

The fast recorded in Jeremiah 36 was to remind the people of
their punishment. Jeremiah tried to counterbalance
Jehoiakim's influence by telling the people what was ahead if
they did not repent.

2D. Different Dating Systems Used

Daniel supposedly erred in stating that Nebuchadnezzar
invaded Palestine in the third year of Jehoiakim. (Jeremiah
25:1 states that Nebuchadnezzar's first year coincided with
Jehoiakim's fourth year.) However, a different dating system
was used in Jerusalem (where Jeremiah wrote his account)
than in Babylon (where Daniel wrote his account).

According to J. D. Wilson, a professor in history: ". . . there
is no need to suggest discrepancy. In the Babylonian calendar
the year began in the spring. In Judah the year began in the
autumn. The Babylonian third year would overlap the
Judean fourth year by about six months. The same date could
be both the third and fourth year, according to the mode of
reckoning." 43/35

Raven notes: ". . . in Assyria and Babylon a king's reign was
usually reckoned from the New Year's day after his accession
but in Judah often from the previous New Year's day
(Hastings B.D. Vol. I. p. 400). Inscriptions in Babylon are
dated in the reign of a king up to the close of the year in
which he died. Daniel naturally follows this Babylonian
method and thus his 'third year of Jehoiakim' is identical
with Jeremiah's 'fourth year.' " 32/320

Waltke notes: "But how can one square the statement made
in Daniel 1:1 that Nebuchadnezzar in his first year as king
besieged Jerusalem in the third year of Jehoiakim with the
statement in Jeremiah 25:1,9; 46:1 that Nebuchadnezzar
defeated Necho in his first year, which is correlated with the
fourth year of Jehoiakim. Edwin Thiele in his work,
Mysterious Numbers of the Hebrew Kings, harmonizes this
conflicting data by proposing that Daniel is using the
Babylonian system of dating the king's reign whereas
Jeremiah is using the Palestinian system of dating. In
Babylonia, the year in which the king ascended the throne
was designated specifically as 'the year of accession to the
kingdom,' and this was followed by the first, second, and
subsequent years of rule. In Palestine, on the other hand,

there was no accession year as such, so that the length of rule was computed differently with the year of accession being regarded as the first year of the king's reign. If this plausible explanation is correct, the alleged contradiction actually supports a sixth century date of the book. Had the author of Daniel been an unknown Jew of the second century B.C., it is unlikely that he would have followed the obsolete Babylonian chronological system of computation in preference to his own Palestinian method, which had the sanction of so important a personage as the prophet Jeremiah." 74/325,326

The critics also object that Daniel 1:1 represents Nebuchadnezzar as the king who besieged Jerusalem when he did not become king until several months later after the death of his father.

Keil suggests that ". . . he who afterwards became king might be proleptically styled king, though he was at the time only the commander of the army." 23/36

Or, as Professor Young says: ". . . the word King is used here proleptically, as we say, 'In the childhood of President Washington.' " 50/356

If Nebuchadnezzar had *set out for* Jerusalem, he must have done so after returning to Babylon upon the death of his father. In that case, he already would have been the king. If he *came to* Jerusalem from his victory at Carchemish, which seems more consistent with Berosus' account, then he was proleptically called king. Belshazzar was in the same situation. While his father was away, Belshazzar was the acting king, and he enjoyed the benefits of kingship. He who exercised the authority of kingship may have been regarded the real ruler.

D. J. Wiseman states: "Whichever solution is accepted there remains the question of the siege of Jerusalem in this year, an event unattested in the Chronicle. It could be argued that since the Babylonian Chronicle recording the events of 605 B.C. is primarily concerned with the major defeat of the Egyptians, a successful incursion into Judah by the Babylonian army group which returned from the Egyptian border could be included in the claim that at that time Nebuchadnezzar conquered 'all Hatti' (i.e. Syria-Palestine). If so, Daniel 1:1 would imply that the Babylonian king was himself present." 47/17,18 This is not improbable since the energy of the young king in leading his troops is attested frequently in the Chronicle.

It appears obvious from Daniel 1:2 that the author had before
him the writings of Jeremiah. If Daniel were written in the
second century B.C., the author surely would not have
deliberately contradicted Jeremiah concerning the
corresponding years of Nebuchadnezzar and Jehoiakim, nor
would he have contradicted the clear statements of II Kings
and II Chronicles concerning the events. But a sixth century
author, not wishing to reiterate in great detail well-known
recent history — ignominious events to the Jews — would
have been prone to give a brief summary and would have felt
free to date the events from his perspective.

7C.   SUMMARY

Concerning the radical critics' belief that Daniel made a
mistake in assigning Nebuchadnezzar's siege of Jerusalem to
Jehoiakim's third year, R. D. Wilson concludes: "Inasmuch as
there are no contemporaneous documents known, which say
one word about the movements of either Nebuchadnezzar, or
Jehoiakim, in the *third* year of the latter king, we may safely rule
this objection out of court. It cannot be too strongly
emphasized that whatever his creed, or learning, or critical
acumen, or insight, the *ipse dixits*, the mere assertions, of any
man with regard to the movements of the kings of the time of
Nebuchadnezzar, are worthy of absolutely no consideration
whatsoever, insofar as they are unsupported by evidence.
What any man thinks about the matter is opinion, not
evidence. Necho, king of Egypt, and all the records of Egypt are
silent about the third year of Jehoiakim. Nabopolassar and
Nebuchadnezzar, kings of Babylon, and the Babylonian
documents of a private as well as of a public character, are silent
about it. The biblical books of Kings, Chronicles, Jeremiah and
Ezekiel, are silent with regard to it. Berosus, the Babylonian
historian, and Josephus, the Jewish historian, who claim to
have had access to contemporaneous documents, support the
statement that Nebuchadnezzar had made an expedition
across the Euphrates a short time before his father
Nabopolassar died; that is, either in the third or fourth year of
Jehoiakim. The writer of Dan. i, I, declares that
Nebuchadnezzar did make an expedition against Jerusalem in
the third year of Jehoiakim. As to this point, the writer of the
book of Daniel, at whatever time it was written, would
probably know more than we do to-day; for *we know nothing*.
No evidence proves nothing. This attack on the veracity of the
writer of the book of Daniel should be ruled out until some
evidence is forthcoming to show that he did not come up
against Jerusalem during this third year of Jehoiakim." 44/81,82

4B. The Chaldeans

1C. THE PROBLEM

The author of the Book of Daniel uses the word "Chaldeans" (*Kasdim*) to denote a special class of wise men. However, the word originally had a broader meaning and referred to a particular group of tribes. The controversy concerns whether the more limited sense of the word was in use in the sixth century B.C.

2C. REPRESENTATIVE CONTENTIONS OF THE RADICAL CRITICS

Driver asserts: "The 'Chaldeans' are synonymous in Daniel (i,4; ii,2; etc.) with the caste of wise men. This sense 'is unknown to the Ass. Bab. language, has, wherever it occurs, formed itself after the end of the Babylonian empire, and is thus an indication of the post-exilic composition of the Book' (Schrader, *The Cuneiform Inscriptions and the Old Testament*, 2nd edition, p. 429). It dates, namely, from a time when practically the only 'Chaldeans' known belonged to the caste in question (comp. Meinhold, *Beiträge*, p. 28)." 12/468

Professor Cornill says: "The manner in which the term *kasdim* (Chaldean), exactly like the Latin Chaldaeus, is used in the sense of soothsayer and astrologer (ii, 2,4,5,10; iv, 4; v, 7,11) is *inconceivable* at a time when the Chaldeans were the ruling people of the world." 55/387

3C. EVALUATING CRITICAL CONTENTIONS

1D. Literary contention: "Chaldeans" is synonymous in Daniel with the caste of wise men.

2D. Philosophical contention: "Chaldean" could not denote soothsayer and astrologer at a time when the Chaldeans ruled that whole area.

3D. Historical contention: This sense is unknown in the Assyrian-Babylonian language.

4D. Deduction: This sense must have formed after the end of the Chaldean empire.

5D. Deduction: This sense dates from a time when the only Chaldeans known were those of the caste of wise men.

6D. Deductive conclusion: Therefore, this use of "Chaldean" indicates the post-exilic composition of Daniel.

4C. QUESTIONS IN DISPUTE

1D. Does Daniel use "Chaldean" to refer exclusively to the caste of master astrologers?

2D. Is there any historical evidence that "Chaldean" also referred to the caste of master astrologers during the period of Chaldean ascendancy?

5C. ANSWERS

1D. History of the Chaldeans

Babylon was an ancient city-state in the plain of Shinar and the capital of Babylonia, the eastern end of the Fertile Crescent. It was the center of intellectual life in western Asia and especially noted for its study of the stars. Thus Babylon became a center for magicians, sorcerers, diviners and other occult practitioners.

The Chaldeans are first mentioned in early Babylonian notices. The name appears in Assyrian notices after 883 B.C. Because of their proficiency in astronomy and skillful practice of astrology, the Chaldeans became a caste of astrologers. They were prominent in Babylonia beginning in 625 B.C.

Thus the Chaldeans could be considered priests because of their involvement with the gods and fates. They acquired special powers from their knowledge of astronomy and their investment in occult magic.

2D. Both Meanings Found in Daniel

Diodorus Siculus (first century B.C.) reports: "The Chaldeans after inhabiting Babylonia for many centuries, as a kind of priestly caste, attained political supremacy through Nabopolassar" (II,26).

They maintained this supremacy until the fall of Babylon to Cyrus. Known as Chaldeans to the Babylonians, these men were considered a special, elevated class because they were priests to Bel. Therefore, it seems likely that this use of the term "Chaldeans" fits Daniel's time. 26/28

The Chaldeans most likely were originally a priestly class which attained ruling status. After losing that status, they still retained their defining characteristic as priests, but priests who for a time possessed political power.

The term "Chaldeans" certainly occurs in both senses in Daniel. Although the word is used seven times in chapters 2, 4 and 5 to refer only to master astrologers, it also is used four times without unconditional reference to the caste of wise men. The reference to the "language of the Chaldeans" (1:4) obviously implies an ethnic or tribal group. The expressions "kingdom of the Chaldeans" (9:1) and "certain Chaldeans" (3:8) also are stripped of identification with astrologers and other wise men.

Archer points out ". . . the author of this work was certainly aware that *Kasdim* was the ethnic term for the race of Nebuchadnezzar. Thus in Daniel 5:30 Belshazzar is referred to as the king of the Chaldeans; in this case the term certainly could not refer to any class of wise men. Therefore, the theory of late origin fails to explain the facts as we have them." 3/382

Joseph Wilson explains: "It is used in both senses in Daniel. See v, 30. It was used in both senses in later times, why could it not have been so used in the time of Daniel? Whatever reason existed for its special use at any time, existed also in Babylon under Nebuchadnezzar. 'But Ezekiel does not use the limited sense, nor does Jeremiah.' Why should they? They had no occasion to refer to the guild so designated. The Chaldeans were the early inhabitants of Southern Mesopotamia. They were distinguished for their learning, especially in arithmetic and astronomy. Their treatises were written in their own tongue, which became a learned tongue in Babylon, just as Greek or Latin is now. And just as we call a scholar a 'Grecian' who understands the Greek language, so they who knew the ancient tongue were termed Chaldeans. Doubtless Daniel himself was one of them, though by birth a Jew. He was sent to school that he might acquire 'the learning and tongue of the Chaldeans,' i,4." 43/57,58

3D.   "Chaldeans" as Special Class Used Early

1E.   Herodotus

From Herodotus (*c.* 450 B.C.) we learn that the use of "Chaldeans" as a special class dates back to Daniel's time. In his *The Histories* (1:181-183), Herodotus refers to his visit to the Chaldeans. He mentions a festival they were having when he arrived and reports what they told him concerning the festival and their temple.

According to E. J. Young, Herodotus regarded the Chaldeans as priests. In addition, the festival they were celebrating during Herodotus' visit was an ancient one, for the Chaldeans told Herodotus that in the time of Cyrus (*c.* 539-530 B.C.) the temple contained a huge gold statue of a man.

Young says: "The natural impression which one receives from these words of Herodotus is that the order of things described had been in existence since the time of Cyrus. The sanctuary had been standing since that time, and it appears to be a justifiable inference that the sanctuary priests, the Chaldeans, had also been in existence since that time." 51/272

J. D. Wilson points out that in all of Herodotus' references to the Chaldeans, he uses no other meaning than an order of priests. This usage, therefore, was well established in Herodotus' time and easily could have dated back to the time of Daniel. 43/58,59

2E.   Derivation of "Chaldean"

A totally different explanation involves the theory that *Kaldu* (Chaldean) is derived from an ancient title.

Archer explains: "Another suggestion has been offered by R. D. Wilson (*Studies in the Book of Daniel*, Series One) to the effect that the Akkadian *Kasdu* or *Kaldu*, referring to a type of priest, was derived from an old Sumerian title *Gal-du* (meaning 'master builder'), a term referring to the building of astronomical charts which were used as an aid to astrological prediction. Wilson cites such a use of *Gal-du* in a tablet from the fourteenth year of Shamash-shumukin of Babylon (668-648 B.C.). It should be noted that a good many Sumerian titles have been found which contain the element *Gal* ('great one,' 'chief,' 'master'). On a single page in Jacobsen's *Copenhagen Texts* (p. 3) we find these titles Gal-LU KUR, Gal-UKÚ, Gal-DAN-QAR, and Gal-SUKKAL. The resemblance between this *Gal-du* or *Kaldu* and the ethnic term *Kaldu* as a by-form of *Kasdu* would be purely accidental. Such an explanation clears up the divergent usages of this term by the author of Daniel." 3/382

In subsequent development of the Babylonian dialect, or Akkadian, the sibilants *s*, *š* and *ş* often changed to *l* before dentals like *t* and *d*. This accounts for the appearances of *Kaldu* rather than *Kasdu*. It later developed in Greek as *Khaldaioi* (Chaldeans). Perhaps Daniel used this title to refer to a caste of wise men, a homonymic reference which also applied to a race of people.

4D.   Not Found in Assyrian-Babylonian Language

Aramaic (formerly referred to as Chaldee) probably includes many words in use at that time which have not yet been found on documents dating from that period. In fact, there is no other document in Aramaic that comes from the late sixth century B.C. The Asshur Letter published by Lidzbarski in 1921 dates from about 650 B.C. The Elephantine Papyri come from 420 to 380 or thereabouts. Daniel is the only sixth century Aramaic literature extant. "Chaldean," in the sense of a caste of wise men, could be one of these words.

Professor Wilson points out: "All analogy, based on records already found, would lead us to believe that hundreds of both native and foreign words were used by the ancient Arameans that have hitherto been discovered in no Aramaic document." 44/323

Raven writes: "It is hard to prove a negative. Our knowledge of the Babylonian literature of the time of Daniel is not so complete that we can safely affirm that 'Chaldean' never meant the caste of wise men in his time. Indeed Schrader says that we are thus far confined to Assyrian sources for our knowledge of the Chaldeans. We are therefore in no position to dispute the true use of the word in the Book of Daniel." 32/321

Young concludes that because there is no other known sixth century B.C. writing using "Chaldean" to refer to a caste of wise men, this in no way indicates that Daniel was written late. 50/357

The radical critics' argument that the use of "Chaldean" as a special caste does not date back to Daniel's time is a purely negative speculation which cannot be proven.

6C. SUMMARY

The radical critics' argument fails to explain the clear ethnic use of the term in Daniel 5:30 and elsewhere. There is clear evidence that the Chaldeans were a caste of priests both during and after the Neo-Babylonian empire. This empire was ruled by people originating from the city-states of Chaldea, just as the Roman empire was ruled by people originating from the city-state of Rome. A perfectly satisfactory explanation for a non-ethnic homonym is found in a Sumerian title applied in all likelihood to astrologer priests. In addition, the critics' argument is based on one negative claim, which in itself proves nothing.

5B. Belshazzar

1C. INTRODUCTION

Daniel states that Belshazzar was king of Babylon. In addition, the book seems to indicate that Belshazzar was the last king and that Nebuchadnezzar was his father. It is known, however, that Nebuchadnezzar was not actually his father. In point of fact, Nabonidus was the last king and Belshazzar was merely his son, even though he may have been recognized as the crown prince.

2C. REPRESENTATIVE CONTENTIONS OF THE RADICAL CRITICS

Driver writes: "Belshazzar is represented as *king* of Babylon; and Nebuchadnezzar is spoken of throughout c. 5 (*vv.* 2. 11. 13.

18. 22) as his *father*. In point of fact, Nabonidus (Nabu-nahid) was the last king of Babylon; he was a usurper, not related to Nebuchadnezzar, and one *Belsharuzur* is mentioned as his son." 12/468

Driver goes on to say: "Though Belshazzar was a historical character, who probably held a prominent position at the time of the capture of the city, it must be owned that the representation given is such as to support somewhat strongly the opinion that it is founded upon the Jewish tradition of a later age." 12/468

Sayce states: "Belshazzar never became king in his father's place." 35/525

3C. EVALUATING CRITICAL CONTENTIONS

   1D. Literary Contentions

      1E. Belshazzar is the king of Babylon in Daniel.

      2E. Nebuchadnezzar is Belshazzar's father in Daniel.

   2D. Historical Contentions

      1E. Nabonidus was the last king of Babylon.

      2E. Nabonidus was usurper of the throne and unrelated to Nebuchadnezzar.

      3E. Nabonidus was the father of Belshazzar.

      4E. Belshazzar never became king in his father's place.

   3D. Deduction: Any representation of Belshazzar as king must stem from later Jewish tradition and not from solid historical evidence.

   4D. Contention: Daniel errs in calling Belshazzar king and the son of Nebuchadnezzar.

4C. THE BABYLONIAN KINGS

A list of the rulers of the Chaldean empire as known from archaeology follows:

Nabopolassar, 625-605 B.C.

Nebuchadnezzar II (son of Nabopolassar), 605-562 B.C.

Evil-Merodach (son of Nebuchadnezzar), 562-560 B.C.

Neriglissar or Nergal-sar-ezer of Jeremiah 39:3 (murdered Evil-Merodach, his brother-in-law), 560-556 B.C.

Labashi-Marduk (son of Neriglissar), 556 B.C. (nine months)

Nabonidus (murdered Labashi-Marduk), 556-539 B.C.

Belshazzar (eldest son of Nabonidus), co-regent or prince-regent with Nabonidus

Jeremiah 27:7 states that "all the nations shall serve him [Nebuchadnezzar], and his son, and his grandson, until the time of his own land comes; then many nations and great kings will enslave him."

5C. QUESTIONS IN DISPUTE

   1D. Why is Nebuchadnezzar called Belshazzar's father?

   2D. Why is Belshazzar called king?

6C. ANSWERS

   1D. Reasons for Genetic Terminology

   With the above considerations in mind, why is Nebuchadnezzar called the father of Belshazzar four times in Daniel 5:2,11,13 and 18, with three different pronouns (his, your, my) attesting to the relationship? Also, in 5:22, Belshazzar is called Nebuchadnezzar's son. The Aramaic word for "son" can also mean "grandson," "descendant" or "offspring." 19/1120

   Concerning the term "father," Archer points out: ". . . it is a distinct possibility that in this case there was a genetic relationship between Nebuchadnezzar and Belshazzar. If Nabonidus married a daughter of Nebuchadnezzar in order to legitimize his usurpation of the throne back in 556 B.C., it would follow that his son by her would be the grandson of Nebuchadnezzar." 3/383

   John Raven adds: "The suggestion that Nabonidus may have strengthened his position as king by marrying a daughter of the great king Nebuchadnezzar is made the more plausible by the fact that he named one of his sons Nebuchadnezzar. In this case Belshazzar was the grandson of Nebuchadnezzar and according to the Hebrew usage could be called his son." 32/321,322; 16/424

   If Nabonidus did this, he followed the precedent set by Neriglissar, who also married one of Nebuchadnezzar's daughters to gain the throne. 43/29

   Gleason Archer suggests an alternative solution as a second option: ". . . by ancient usage the term son often referred to a successor in the same office whether or not there was a blood relationship." 3/382,383

   Belshazzar thus could be called Nebuchadnezzar's "son" in the sense of being his successor on the throne.

2D.   Reasons for Kingship Terminology

Archaeology has shown that Nabonidus took up residence at
Teima (Teman) in North Arabia and left Belshazzar in charge
of the northern frontier of the Babylonian empire. Thus,
Belshazzar became the *de facto* king of Babylon, or sub-king.

Young believes that "Belshazzar then, technically occupied a
position subordinate to that of Nabonidus. Nevertheless,
since he was the man *in regal status* with whom the Jews had
to do, Daniel calls him king. This cannot justly be charged as
an inaccuracy." 50/359

Some scholars believe, however, that Belshazzar was more
than a sub-king. Charles Boutflower states: "At the same
time it is more likely that in Dan. v. 1 the royal title is given to
Belshazzar in the higher sense, either as sharing the supreme
power, along with his father, or as the *de facto* king." 4/118

Waltke explains: "The appearance of King Belshazzar in
chapter 5 was interpreted by earlier critics to be unhistorical
inasmuch as all the classic historians presented Nabonidus
as the last king of Babylon and never mentioned Belshazzar.
However, after comparing the statements of Daniel 5 with
the cuneiform evidence that later became available, R. P.
Dougherty came to the firm conclusion that the view that the
chapter originated in the Maccabean period was thoroughly
discreditable. These archaeological discoveries show that for
much of the reign of Nabonidus, his eldest son Belshazzar
acted as co-regent. When Nabonidus took up residence in
Teima, Belshazzar exercised sole rule in Babylonia, and for
this reason was represented as the last king of Babylon in
Daniel (Daniel 5:30). (See R. P. Dougherty, *Nabonidus and
Belshazzar*, pp. 59 ff., 194.)" 74/328

E. J. Young points out that the Aramaic word translated
"king" (*malka*) does not necessarily mean an absolute
monarch. 50/368

Boutflower reports: "In the Annalistic Tablet, from the
seventh year of Nabonidus onward, we are confronted year
by year with the statement, 'The king was in Temâ, the king's
son,' *i.e.* Belshazzar, 'the *nobles* and the soldiers were in the
country of Akkad.' In very much the same light is Belshazzar
brought before us in the opening verse of Dan. v.:
'Belshazzar the king made a great feast to a thousand of his
lords,' where the Aramaic word translated 'lords' comes from
a kindred root to that translated 'nobles' on the tablet." 4/120

Boutflower summarizes: "We must remember that for at least
ten of the seventeen years of Nabonidus the defence of the

country had rested on Belshazzar, while his father
Nabonidus lived in retirement at Temâ. Also, that on the
night of that fatal feast the person of Nabonidus had been in
the hands of the enemy for well-nigh four months, so that
during that interval in the eyes of the world at large
Belshazzar would appear as the actual ruler. At any rate he
would so appear in the eyes of the author of the Book of
Daniel, writing after the event was over. For him, the reign of
Nabonidus would end with his capture and he would view
Belshazzar as the last of the Neo-Babylonian kings." 4/118

In several building inscriptions, Nabonidus associates
Bel-shar-usur (Belshazzar) with himself in such a way that
indicates Belshazzar took an active part in the government as
a co-regent. 19/1120

For example: "Life for long days give as a gift to me; and as
for Bel-shar-usur, my first born, the offspring of my body,
may the reverence for thy great godhead be placed in his
heart. May he not contract sin. May he be sated with the
fulness of life." 25/246

This prayer is significant because such prayers customarily
were made only for the reigning monarch. Nabonidus thus
associates Belshazzar with himself on the throne. 3/383

Sir Henry Rawlinson noted (as referred to by George
Rawlinson, professor of ancient history at Canterbury in
1972) that the Babylonian monarchs' custom was not to
mention family members in public documents unless they
were inseparably associated with them in their reign.
Belshazzar thus would be mentioned because of his
position.

Archer says: "Still other cuneiform documents attest that
Belshazzar presented sheep and oxen at the temples in
Sippar as 'an offering of the king.' " 3/383

The Persian Verse Account, discovered by Sidney Smith,
proves that Belshazzar did rule as king in Babylon in his
father's absence. Smith depicts the events concerning
Nabonidus' expedition to Teima as follows:

"He (Nabonidus) put the eldest, his firstborn, in charge of a
    camp.
The troops of the land he sent with him.
He freed his hand; he entrusted the kingship to him,
while he himself set out on a distant campaign.
The forces of Akkad advanced with him.
Towards Tema, in Amurru, he set his face." 37/88; 11/106 ff.

About this account Gruenthauer says: "From this passage it

is apparent that Nabonidus conferred royal powers upon Belshazzar in the third year of his reign. . . . Charles in an over-cautious mood, expresses some doubt as to whether the son of the king mentioned in the Chronicle is Belshazzar on the ground that Nabonidus had other sons. But the Persian Verse Account excludes every vestige of doubt: it states explicitly that the son to whom the kingship was entrusted was Nabonidus' firstborn." 16/417

T. G. Pinches has deciphered a cuneiform tablet found at Erech, which says: "Ishi-Amurru, son of Nuranu, has sworn by Bel, Nebo, the lady of Erech, and Nana, the oath of Nabonidus king of Babylon and of Belshazzar the king's son, that on the 7th day of the month Adar of the twelfth year of Nabonidus king of Babylon I will go to Erech." 4/119

Concerning this tablet Pinches observes: "The importance of this inscription is that it places Belshazzar practically on the same plane as Nabonidus his father, five years before the latter's deposition, and the bearing of this will not be overlooked. Officially Belshazzar had not been recognised as king, as this would have necessitated his father's abdication, but it seems clear that he was in some way associated with his father on the throne, otherwise his name would hardly have been introduced into the oath with which the inscription begins. We now see that not only for the Hebrews, but also for the Babylonians, Belshazzar held a practically royal position." 62/297-299; 4/119

It was a common practice in ancient times for the king to appoint a sub-king over part of his kingdom. Gruenthauer says: "For we know from the inscriptions of Nergal-shar-usur that Bel-shum-ishkun was king of Babylon during the reign of Nebuchadnezzar. Still his name does not appear upon any contract tablet. Nergal-shar-usur calls him 'King of Babylon' without adding any qualification whatever to indicate that he was only a sub-king under Nebuchadnezzar." 16/416; 25/210,1.14; 214,1.11

If Bel-shum-ishkun was sub-king under Nebuchadnezzar, Belshazzar could have held a similar position.

Later, when Cyrus conquered Babylon, he appointed his son Cambyses "king of Babylon." Boutflower states: "It is reasonable, therefore, to suppose that Belshazzar bore the same title that was afterwards given to Cambyses." 4/118

The critics are hesitant to accept this final evidence. They point out that Belshazzar is always referred to as "the son of the king" in the inscriptions, that his name appears on no contract tablets and that Nabonidus is called "king of

Babylon" without any indication that Belshazzar was sub-king (unlike the double references to Cyrus and Cambyses on the contract tablets). But these arguments are inconclusive.

R. H. Pfeiffer concedes: "We shall presumably never know how our author learned that the new Babylon was the creation of Nebuchadnezzar (4:30 [H. 4:27]), as the excavations have proved (see R. Koldewey, *Excavations at Babylon*, 1915), and that Belshazzar, mentioned only in Babylonian records, in Daniel, and in Bar. 1:11, which is based on Daniel, was functioning as king when Cyrus took Babylon in 538 (ch. 5)." 27/758,759

The radical critics argue, however, that Belshazzar's authority in Daniel chapter 5 to appoint anyone he pleased as third ruler in the kingdom indicates he was an absolute ruler, not a sub-king. Therefore, the author apparently did not know about Nabonidus. Just the opposite is true, however. Why did Belshazzar only promise the third and not the second ruler? Since Nabonidus his father and first ruler was still alive it's rather obvious he could only offer the third to someone else; Belshazzar himself was still the second ruler.

7C. SUMMARY

We have confirmed Belshazzar's status as descendant of Nebuchadnezzar, either by birth or through succession to the same office, and as sub-king under Nabonidus.

6B. Darius the Mede

1C. INTRODUCTION

H. H. Rowley says: "The references to Darius the Mede in the book of Daniel have long been recognized as providing the most serious historical problem in the book." 68/9

D. J. Wiseman expresses what Daniel records: "The Bible clearly declares that after the death of the Chaldean king Belshazzar 'Darius the Mede received the kingdom, being about sixty-two years old' (Dn. 5:30-31). This Darius was 'son of Ahasuerus, of the seed of the Medes, who became king over the realm of the Chaldeans' (9:1). . . . Daniel held a position of authority at least during the first regnal year in Babylon of this king (6:1; 9:1) and, according to the traditional translation of 6:28, 'Daniel prospered during the reign of Darius and the reign of Cyrus the Persian.' Thus Darius the Mede appears to have been succeeded by Cyrus and this verse is considered 'the clearest evidence of the book's belief in a Median empire between the Babylonian and the Persian.' " 47/9

The radical critics claim Daniel's references to Darius the Mede

imply that the author believed a Median kingdom, under
Darius, conquered Babylon and subsequently gave way to the
Persian empire under Cyrus. The critics believe Darius the
Mede did not actually exist — he was a confused reflection of
the later Darius Hystaspes. It is known, however, that the
Babylonian empire fell directly to Cyrus and the Persians, not
to the Medes.

2C. REPRESENTATIVE CONTENTIONS OF THE RADICAL
     CRITICS

Driver evaluates Darius the Mede as follows: "Darius, son of
Ahasuerus, a *Mede*, after the death of Belshazzar, is 'made king
over the realm of the Chaldeans' (5, 31. 6, 1 ff. 9, 1. 11, 1). There
seems to be no room for such a ruler. According to all other
authorities, Cyrus is the immediate successor of Nabu-nahid,
and the ruler of the entire Persian empire. It has been
conjectured that Darius may have been an under-king —
perhaps either identical with the Cyaxares II. of Xenophon, or a
younger brother of Astyages — whom Cyrus may have made
governor of Babylon. In 6, 1, however, where he organises the
empire in 120 satrapies, and in 6, 25, he seems to be
represented as absolute ruler of the Babylonian empire,
without any such limitation to his jurisdiction. And in 6, 1 the
temptation to suspect a confusion with Darius *Hystaspis* is
strong." 12/468,469

According to Prince (*Commentary on Daniel*, pp. 54,127), " 'the
author of Daniel had an entirely false idea regarding the fall of
Babylon under the Semitic dynasty. He evidently thought that
Darius the Mede preceded Cyrus the Persian.' The author of
Daniel 'makes a Median ruler receive Babylon after the
overthrow of the native dynasty, and then mentions later the
historical Cyrus. We may suppose that the biblical writer
believed that Cyrus succeeded to the empire of Babylon on the
death of the Median Darius.' "

3C. EVALUATING CRITICAL CONTENTIONS

  1D. Interpretations

    1E. The author of Daniel says a Median ruler received the
         Neo-Babylonian empire after the overthrow of the native
         dynasty.

    2E. The author of Daniel says Darius the Mede preceded Cyrus
         the Persian.

  2D. Assertions

    1E. The author of Daniel thought Cyrus became the ruler of the
         empire after Darius the Mede died.

2E. The author of Daniel thought an independent Median empire existed between the Babylonian and Persian empires.

3E. Darius the Mede does not fit into this period of history.

3D. Contentions

1E. The author of Daniel must have confused Darius the Mede with Darius Hystaspes.

2E. The author of Daniel erred in regard to the fall of Babylon.

4C. QUESTIONS

What does the Book of Daniel say about:

1. When Cyrus became ruler?
2. The identity of Darius and the empire he ruled?

5C. ANSWERS

1D. References to the Medes Are Correct

R. K. Harrison relates: "According to many critical scholars the author of Daniel followed the erroneous precedent of Isaiah (13:17; 21:2) and Jeremiah (51:11,28), according to which the Medes were the sole conquerors of Babylon in 539 B.C., as they had been of Nineveh in 612 B.C. How this theory could ever have arisen is somewhat of a mystery, since one of the Isaiah references (21:2) speaks explicitly of Elam and Media as the joint-conquerors of Babylon, a point that was conceded by Rowley. Be that as it may, archaeological discoveries have shown that it was quite legitimate for Isaiah and Jeremiah to refer to the Medes as the conquerors of Babylon." 19/1128,1129

Some critics claim that Daniel is at fault for referring to the Medes because by the time of Cyrus they had been absorbed into the Persian empire. However, this accusation is unfounded. In his study of the cuneiform on the Harran *Stele*, D. J. Wiseman has shown there are explicit references to the "king of the Medes," even after the assimilation of the Medes into the Persian empire. Also, as a part of the Persian empire, the Medes were under the authority of Cyrus. 19/1129

Many critics believe Daniel 1:2 reflects II Chronicles 36:6,7. In addition, Daniel 1:21 seems to parallel II Chronicles 36:20. But II Chronicles 36:20 implicitly excludes an intervening Median kingdom. It states, in reference to Nebuchadnezzar, that "they [the Jews] were servants to him and to his sons until the rule of the kingdom of Persia." If the author of

Daniel were writing in the second century B.C., as the critics claim, he would have been familiar with this passage in the Old Testament and hardly would have contradicted this source. (Actually, as noted in chapter 2, the fact that Daniel mentions the Medes before the Persians is evidence for the book's early composition. In later times the order was usually reversed, as in "Persia and Media.") 42/55

2D.   History of Media and Persia

The Medes and Persians were two Aryan tribes from the western end of the Iranian plateau. Media was south of the Caspian Sea, and Persia was south of Media by the Persian Gulf.

The Assyrian empire dominated the Medes until near the end of the seventh century B.C. As Assyrian power lessened, the Medes grew stronger until, in alliance with Nabopolassar the Chaldean, they captured Nineveh, the Assyrian capital. The Median kingdom reached the height of its power during Nebuchadnezzar's reign. During this period, Media dominated Persia.

About 559 B.C., Cyrus II became the Persian ruler. He defeated the Median overlords and quickly extended his conquests. Media, however, remained an important province within the Persian realm. In 539 B.C., Cyrus defeated Babylon and established the Persian empire over an area that included Palestine and the Fertile Crescent.

Therefore, a Median empire existed during the time of Nebuchadnezzar, but by Belshazzar's reign Persia dominated the Medes.

The critics insist that the author of Daniel wrongly inserts an independent Median empire between the downfall of Babylon and the emergence of Persia under Cyrus. This would make the four kingdoms of Daniel's visions (chapters 2 and 7) Babylon, Media, Persia and Greece.

For several reasons, this view cannot be supported:

1.   The Book of Daniel never claims that Darius is the king of Media, an independent empire, but that he is of Median descent. 50/361,362

Wilson remarks: "The statement that Darius was a Mede no more proves that he was king of Media than does the statement that Napoleon was a Corsican proves that he was king of Corsica. Besides he may have been a king of Media and still have been a subordinate to Cyrus king of Persia. For example, Murat was a Frenchman who was made king of

Naples and was subordinate to a Corsican Italian who had become emperor of the French." 45/261

2. The author of Daniel says that Darius and Cyrus had different ancestries (*i.e.*, Cyrus the Persian, Darius the Mede), not that they ruled separate kingdoms.

3. According to the critics, Daniel 5:28 indicates that Babylon is to fall partially to the Medes and partially to the Persians. But immediately after this, Darius the Mede is said to be limited by "the law of the Medes and Persians." The author obviously regarded Medo-Persia a unit. If Darius is the king of an independent Median empire, why is he subject to the laws of the Persians? 50/361,362; 3/384,385

4. In addition, Daniel's interpretation of the handwriting on the wall (Daniel 5:25-28) indicates that the author regarded the Persians as the main element of the empire that would succeed the Babylonians. His interpretation of the third word as *peres*, the singular of *parsin*, is a play on words. *Peres* is derived from a word meaning "to divide." Moreover, *peres* points to another word, *Parās*, which means "Persians." The author obviously regarded the Babylonian empire as conquered not by the Medes alone, but by the Medes *and* Persians, with Persia being the more important. 3/398,399

5. The prophecy in Daniel 8 also shows that Daniel did not believe an independent Median empire conquered Babylon. Verse 20 explains that the ram with two horns (8:3,4) represents the Medo-Persian empire. One of the horns — apparently representing the Persians — comes up last. This longer horn appears *before* the ram butts north, west and south to conquer. 5/251; 51/168

   Thus, the Persians ascended to full power over Media before beginning their conquests.

3D. External Traces of Darius

What historical confirmation is there for Darius the Mede? The radical critics customarily proclaim that no evidence exists. In answer to this, J. D. Wilson replies: "But Darius the Mede is not so invisible among ancient writers as the critics would have us suppose. Xenophon says that a Mede succeeded to the throne of Babylon. He gives him the name of Cyaxares. Xenophon's account is romantic and the name he gives cannot be reconciled with other statements. Still, he apparently sees no improbability in a Mede occupying the throne.

"Aeschylus in his *Persae* mentions a Mede as the first leader, followed by Cyrus.

"Abydenus puts in the mouth of Nebuchadnezzar an oracular declaration — 'O Babylonians, I, Nebuchadnezzar announce to you a future calamity. There shall come a Persian mule using our divinities as allies. He shall bring us into bondage; leagued with him shall be the Mede, the boast of Assyria.'

"While these are but faint traces, there occurs in the scholiast upon Aristophanes this statement, 'The Daric (*i.e.* the coin) is not named from Darius (Hystaspis) the father of Xerxes, but from another preceding King.' This preceding King must be Darius the Mede." 43/56

Sir Robert Anderson relates another possible trace of Darius. It concerns the decree Cyrus made to the Jews, promising them safe return to Jerusalem and aid to rebuild the temple. Ezra 6:1-3 states that this decree was found in Achmetha, the capital of Media, instead of the Persian capital at Susa. Anderson asserts that when things returned to normal order, Darius the Mede, who temporarily was governor of Babylon, withdrew from his post to make room for Cyrus and his son Cambyses. When leaving, Darius took all official papers home with him to Achmetha. 20/144,145

4D. Negative Evidence Not Substantial

Raven says that although the name "Darius the Mede" has not been found in the ancient inscriptions, this does not indicate that he did not exist. The critics made the same objections concerning Belshazzar and Sargon (Isaiah 20:1), whose existence has since been proven by archaeology. 32/322

The radical critics admit there is no solid proof against Daniel's account of Darius the Mede. S. L. Driver states: "Still the circumstances are not perhaps such as to be absolutely inconsistent with either the existence or the office of 'Darius the Mede;' and a cautious criticism will not build too much on the silence of the inscriptions, where many certainly remain yet to be brought to light." 12/469

A. B. Rhodes, another critic who believes Daniel was written in the second century B.C., withholds final judgment concerning Darius, admitting that "all the facts may not yet be available."

5D. Possible Solutions

The problem concerns the identity of Darius the Mede. The following lists the rulers of the Persian empire, in order:

Cyrus II (the Great), 559-530 B.C.

Cambyses II, 530-522 B.C.

Darius I (Hystaspes the Great), 522-486 B.C.

Ahasuerus (Xerxes), 486-465 B.C.

Artaxerxes I, 464-423 B.C.

Darius II, 423-404 B.C.

Where does Darius the Mede fit into this list? There seem to be three possibilities.

1. The writer of Daniel, confused about the chronology of the Persian rulers, refers to Darius I as Darius the Mede.

2. Darius the Mede was Cyrus.

3. Darius the Mede was an early governor of Babylon under Cyrus.

Daniel 5:31 and 9:1 do not say that Darius ruled the Persian empire. In 5:31, Darius received the kingdom (of the slain Chaldean king), and in 9:1, Darius was made king over the kingdom of the Chaldeans. Both references indicate that Darius took control of the conquered Chaldean empire, not the Persian empire.

1E.   Darius I (Hystaspes)

The critics believe that Daniel's Darius the Mede is the result of historical confusion. The author confused him with the ruler who followed Cyrus and Cambyses, Darius the son of Hystaspes, who was a Persian, not a Mede.

Harrison replies that "Any suggestion to the effect that the writer placed Darius I before Cyrus and made Xerxes [Ahasuerus] the father of Darius I (cf. Dan. 6:28; 7:1) ignores the fact that Daniel was referring to Darius the Mede. It is difficult to see how an intelligent second-century B.C. Jewish author could possibly have made such blunders as the critical scholars have ascribed to the compiler of Daniel, particularly if he had access to the writings of Ezra. Had the work contained as many frank errors as are usually credited to it, it is certain that the book would never have gained acceptance into the canon of Scripture, since it would have emerged very poorly by comparison with the writings of secular historians such as Herodotus, Ctesias, Menander, and others whose compositions are no longer extant." 19/122

There are three reasons the author of Daniel is not referring to Darius the son of Hystaspes:

1. The author calls him a Mede. It was well known to the ancients that Darius Hystaspes was a Persian.

2. The author states that Darius the Mede was 62 years old when he received the kingdom. It was well known that Darius Hystaspes was fairly young when he began his rule.

3. Daniel 9:1 indicates by the word *homlak* ("was made king") that Darius the Mede was appointed king over Babylon by some higher authority. Darius Hystaspes, however, succeeded to the throne on the death of Cambyses. He immediately had to suppress revolts against Persia in all the outlying dominions of the empire, including Babylon and Media. Thus, *homlak* hardly can refer to Darius Hystaspes, who was certainly the leading authority, not someone appointed by a higher authority. This means that Cyrus must have installed Darius the Mede as governor in Babylon. 3/371,372

J. C. Whitcomb summarizes the reasons the confusion theory fails: "This theory, so firmly entrenched in the thinking of modern critics, suffers fatal blows from the following considerations: (1) even the critics admit that the author of the Book of Daniel must have been a brilliant scholar; (2) the author gives every indication that he intended Darius the Mede to be understood as an historical character; (3) no brilliant Jew of the Maccabean Age could have been as ignorant of Neo-Babylonian and Persian history as the 'reflection hypothesis' demands; (4) there are various ways of showing that the author did not believe in the existence of an independent Median kingdom between the Fall of Babylon and the rise of Persia; (5) if the author were as ignorant of history as the critics claim, the Jews of the Maccabean Age would never have accepted this book as canonical; and (6) the author gives evidence of having a more accurate knowledge of Neo-Babylonian history than any ancient historian since the sixth century B.C." 42/65,66

2E. Cyrus

D. J. Wiseman, professor of assyriology at the University of London, has concluded that Darius the Mede is another name for Cyrus the Persian. In the Harran *Stele* and other sources, Cyrus is called king of the Medes. Also, in Theodotion's ancient text of Bel and the Dragon, the king who sends Daniel to the lions' den is Cyrus of Persia; in the Book of Daniel, it is Darius the Mede. 5/247 (However, even a superficial reading of Bel and the Dragon shows it to be a fictitious account having little correlation, if any, with actual historical events.)

Wiseman explains: "The basis of the hypothesis is that Daniel 6:28 can be translated 'Daniel prospered in the reign of Darius, even (namely, or i.e.) the reign of Cyrus the Persian.' Such a use of the appositional or explicative Hebrew *wāw* construction has long been recognized in I Chronicles 5:26 ('So the God of Israel stirred up the spirit of Pul king of Assyria, even the spirit of Tiglath-pileser king of Assyria') and elsewhere." 47/12

Now is the time to look at the exact content of the references in Daniel to Darius the Mede and Cyrus the Persian:

5:31, "Darius the Mede received the kingdom at about the age of sixty-two."

6:28, "Daniel enjoyed success in the reign of Darius and in the reign of Cyrus the Persian."

9:1, "In the first year of Darius, the son of Ahasuerus, of Median descent, who was made king over the kingdom of the Chaldeans . . ."

10:1, "In the third year of Cyrus king of Persia . . ."

If Darius and Cyrus are the same person, why are they distinctly called Darius the Mede and Cyrus the Persian within such a close space in the historical narrative (5:31; 6:28)? Also, in the prophetic section of Daniel, a clear distinction is made between Darius of Median descent, who was made king over the kingdom of the Chaldeans (9:1), and Cyrus, who was king of Persia (10:1). They hardly can be the same individual.

Wiseman states: "If it is argued that a contemporary writer would not refer to one and the same person by such distinct names as Cyrus the Persian and Darius the Mede, then it must be pointed out that the use of the different names applies to clearly defined sections of the book (5:30 - 6:28; 9 and 11-12) which are given a single date ('the first year of Darius'). Further investigation might disclose some reason for this peculiarity or literary preference." 47/16

This reference to the sections of Daniel which are given a single date is clearly in error, for these reasons:

1. The reference in 11:1 to the "first year of Darius the Mede" is part of an incidental flashback mentioned by the angel. The material which precedes and follows this reference is not related to it chronologically.

2. A simple analysis of Daniel's structure shows that the first six chapters are a chronological account of Daniel's

interpretations of Nebuchadnezzar's dreams and of his significant interactions with the Chaldeans; the last six chapters relate Daniel's prophetic dreams and visions in the order that God gave them to him.

3. The events that follow the first few verses of chapter six do not necessarily fall within the first year of Darius.

In conclusion, Wiseman writes: "It is submitted that, while it must remain only a theory and be further tested, the view that the 'Darius the Mede' could be another name used of 'Cyrus the Persian' and as such specifically noted in Daniel 6:28 has support from the text itself in that Cyrus was about sixty-two years old, received the kingdom and appointed governors. Since he was probably known to Nabonidus, his second cousin, as 'king of the Medes,' a claim to Median descent as echoed by some classical writers is not impossible. As in the case of the Gubaru theory, there is as yet no clear evidence for or against the claim that Cyrus was a 'son of Xerxes,' or that he bore another name. That kings in the ancient near east bore more than one name is abundantly attested." 47/15,16

But the notion that Cyrus was about 62 years old when he conquered Babylon is highly speculative. Cyrus was killed in battle six years later. If he were 62 when he conquered Babylon, he would have been leading his troops in battle at the age of 68, which seems highly improbable.

Furthermore, why would Cyrus be known as "king of the Medes"? Cyrus came from Persia, not Media, and Persia under Cyrus had overthrown the Median rulers and conquered not only Media but also Elam, the third important province in that area.

Bulman explains how Darius and Cyrus can be related by descent: "Darius was 'the son of Ahasuerus, of the seed of the Medes' (9:1). The sources are not always consistent in reporting Cyrus's ancestry. Attention will be given here only to the testimony allowing the correspondence. Josephus [*Antiquities* X,11,4] departs from Daniel by saying that Darius was the son of Astyages — hardly intending to contradict Daniel, but rather to identify Ahasuerus, perhaps a dynastic title, with Astyages. According to Herodotus [*Histories* I,108] and Xenophon [*Cyropaedia*, I,ii,1], Cyrus, whose paternal ancestry was Persian, on his maternal side was the grandson of the Median king Astyages. If Josephus and these Greek writers were talking about the same Astyages, who is thus to be identified with Ahasuerus, then Cyrus was the 'son' of Ahasuerus in the sense in which this word is several times used in the Bible — as a descendant. Moreover, according to Josephus's testimony here, Darius was a descendant of one who had the same name, 'Astyages,' as one of whom Cyrus, according to these Greek writers, was a descendant.

"To speak of Cyrus as Median would seem all the more appropriate since Astyages was without male issue and the Median kingdom was acquired by Cyrus. Aeschylus [*Persae*, 766-773] omits Cyrus's Persian ancestry and puts him in the line of Median kings, and apparently as the legal heir of Astyages. Also, *Bel and the Dragon* describes the kingdom of Astyages as inherited by Cyrus (1:1)." 5/263,264

Although Cyrus may have been the grandson of the Median king Astyages and thus in the line of Median descent, this does not necessarily identify Ahasuerus, father of Darius, with Astyages of Media. There is no reference in Daniel to Cyrus the Mede. Cyrus the Persian and Darius the Mede seem to be distinct and separate entities.

Also, concerning the reference in Bel and the Dragon, it is known that Cyrus conquered Astyages, king of the Medes. Unless "inherited" is meant in the sense of "to conquer," the author of Bel and the Dragon is in error.

This seems *in toto* a fallacious line of reasoning.

3E. Governor of Babylon (Gubaru)

The only real alternative seems to be that Darius the Mede was appointed governor of the conquered Chaldean provinces.

The critics contend that Darius the Mede displays too much authority (in Daniel 6:25) to be only a governor. However, the word translated "earth" in "all the earth" can also mean "land" or "country." This Aramaic word, *'ar 'a*, therefore, presents no problem since it can denote the land over which Cyrus gave him control. It also is possible that he was following the ancient custom of Babylonian kings to speak in terms implying universal dominion. 3/372

Archer explains why Darius might have given the command in Daniel 6:25: "In view of the intimate connection between religious and political loyalty which governed the attitude of the peoples of that ancient culture, it might well have been considered a statesmanlike maneuver to compel all the diverse inhabitants with their heterogeneous tribal and religious loyalties to acknowledge in a very practical way the supremacy of the new Persian empire which had taken over supreme control of their domains. A temporary suspension of worship (at least in the sense of presenting petitions for blessing and aid) was a measure well calculated to convey to the minds of Darius' subjects the reality of the change in control from the overlordship of the Chaldeans to that of the Medes and Persians. In the light of ancient psychology, therefore, it is unwarrantable to rule out of possibility such a remarkable decree or to condemn it as fabulous or unhistorical, as many critics have done." 3/386

In answer to the objection that Darius as governor would not have the power to divide the Babylonian empire into 120 satrapies, Young says: "But the text of Daniel does not say that the kingdom was organized into 120 satrapies, only that Darius appointed 120 satraps (kingdom-protectors) throughout his kingdom. These men have been given the special mission of caring for the newly conquered country, because of the hostility of the land to the conquerors. It may have been, in other words, merely a temporary arrangement and not a formal organization of the country into 120 satrapies. And the satraps may have had responsibility over districts that were smaller in size than actual satrapies. Some of them may merely have been appointed to special mission. . . . There simply is not extant any objective evidence which will justify one in denying the statements of 6:1. For that matter, even if the text did say that the kingdom was divided into 120 satrapies, such a statement could not be shown to be in error." 50/368,369

The name "Darius the Mede" does not appear in ancient literature. If he was governor of Babylon, what was his identity? Many scholars identify him with a governor named Gubaru.

Whitcomb says: "It is true that the name 'Darius the Mede' has not yet been found in any extra-Biblical inscription of pre-Christian times. Nevertheless, Gubaru the Governor of Babylon fits the Biblical description of Darius the Mede so remarkably that the writer believes he will be recognized in due time as the monarch who played such an important role in the life of Daniel after the Fall of Babylon." 42/66

Cuneiform records and Greek historians testify to this man's importance in Babylon's capture and as its first governor under Cyrus.

For a long time a man named Ugbaru of ancient inscriptions was identified with Gubaru. Whitcomb shows that they are two different people and thus resolves the apparent discrepancies in the ancient records. He reports: "Sidney Smith's new translation of the Nabonidus Chronicle in 1924, plus the publication of additional Babylonian contract tablets bearing the name of Gubaru, made it possible for the first time to see the error of the earlier 'Gobryas' identification. Now it became evident that Ugbaru, not Gubaru, was the Governor of Gutium who conquered Babylon, and that this Ugbaru could not possibly be the great Governor of Babylon mentioned in the same Nabonidus Chronicle and in the later contract tablets because he died only three weeks after the Fall of Babylon in 539 B.C. The Assyrian 'Gobryas' of Xenophon may well have been the Ugbaru of the Nabonidus Chronicle. In thus separating Ugbaru the Governor of Gutium from Gubaru the Governor of Babylon, the way is opened for identifying Darius the Mede with Gubaru the Governor of Babylon." 42/65

Many radical critics, such as H. H. Rowley, have rejected this identification because of some apparent discrepancies in the ancient records concerning Ugbaru. 3/372

Concerning these objections, especially those of Rowley, R. K. Harrison writes: "Unfortunately Rowley's attempt to introduce clarity into a hitherto obscure situation was vitiated by the fact that his entire position was based upon arguments from inadequate and misleading secondary sources that failed to draw a distinction between Ugbaru and Gubaru. Thus his conclusions must be regarded at best as highly subjective and historically unreliable." 19/1122

Whitcomb concludes: "It is our conviction that Gubaru, the governor of Babylon and the region beyond the river, appears in the book of Daniel as Darius the Mede, the monarch who took charge of the Chaldean kingdom immediately following the death of Belshazzar, and who appointed satraps and presidents (including Daniel) to assist him in the governing of this extensive territory with its many peoples. We believe that this identification is the only one which satisfactorily harmonizes the various lines of evidence which we find in the book of Daniel and in the contemporary cuneiform records." 42/24

6C.   SUMMARY

We have shown that:

1. The author of Daniel did not believe an independent Median empire intervened between the Babylonian and Persian empires.

2. History contains some evidence that Darius the Mede existed.

3. Darius the Mede is not Darius Hystaspes or Cyrus the Great.

4. It is possible to identify Darius the Mede with Gubaru, governor of Babylon.

7B.   "Observed in the Books"

1C.   THE PROBLEM

Daniel 9:2 comments that Daniel "observed in the books the number of the years which was revealed as the word of the Lord to Jeremiah." The radical critics claim "the books" refers to a sacred collection of Scriptures. Such a collection did not exist in the sixth century B.C.

2C.   REPRESENTATIVE CONTENTIONS OF THE RADICAL CRITICS

S. R. Driver deduces: "In 9,2 it is stated that Daniel 'understood by *the books*' the number of years for which, according to Jeremiah, Jerusalem should lie waste. The expression used implies that the prophecies of Jeremiah formed part of a *collection* of sacred books, which nevertheless, it may safely be affirmed, was not formed in 536 B.C." 12/469

Charles (*Century Bible*, "Daniel," p. 95) writes: "The books here are the sacred books, *i.e.* the Scriptures. The phrase implies the formation of a definite collection of Old Testament books." 32/323

3C.   EVALUATING CRITICAL CONTENTIONS

1D.   Daniel refers to "the books," which included Jeremiah's prophecy.

2D.   Daniel must have meant a collection of sacred books.

3D.   Such a collection did not exist in the sixth century B.C., but did exist in the second century B.C.

4C.   QUESTION IN DISPUTE

What are the books that Daniel mentions?

5C.   ANSWERS

Boutflower notes that the Hebrew word translated "books" is *sepher*. Although it can mean "books," that is not its primary meaning. Nowhere is it used as a collection of sacred books.

"According to F. Brown's Hebrew Lexicon *sēpher* is a loan-word answering to the Assyrian *shipru*, which comes from the root *shapâru*, 'to send.' Hence its primary meaning is 'a missive'; then, 'a letter' from some king, prophet, or other influential person; finally 'document,' 'deed,' 'writing,' 'book.' "4/284

Boutflower adds: "In the Book of Jeremiah, with which the passage in Dan. ix.2 is concerned, *sēpher* is used of law deeds, of a 'book' or collection of written prophecies, and also of prophetic 'missives' or 'letters.' Since there are two prophecies in the Book of Jeremiah concerning the seventy years' captivity, the word might be translated here 'the writings,' viz. of that prophet. Or, again, since the plural is sometimes used of a single letter — cf. Isa. xxxvii.14, also 1 Kings xxi. 8 and 2 Chr. xxxii.17 in R.V.M. — the reference may be to the particular 'letter' given in Jer. xxix. 1-20, which contains one of those prophecies." 4/285

Raven gives this view: "This expression does not necessitate a canon any more than Isaiah 8:16-20 or 34:16. It simply implies that Daniel had in his possession the sacred books so far as they were in existence and in particular Jeremiah who foretold the seventy years of exile (Jer. 25:11-12; 29:10)." 32/323

Young makes the following observation: ". . . to deduce from this that the canon was already formed is to be guilty of a *non-sequitur.* The expression 'by the books' (bassefarim) simply refers to a group of writings among which were also the prophecies of Jeremiah. The term is probably a broad designation of the Scriptures." 50/360

Whatever the proper translation, the books that the author refers to include the writings of Jeremiah. What other Scriptures may have been included is not known.

6C. SUMMARY

"The books" can be understood to mean simply a group of writings that contained Jeremiah's prophecies.

chapter 4
Attacks on Daniel
as a Writer

4A. LINGUISTIC ARGUMENTS

The Book of Daniel was composed in two different languages.
Aramaic was used from the fourth verse of the second chapter to the
end of the seventh chapter. The rest of the book is composed in
Hebrew. Like all languages, Aramaic and Hebrew have changed
over the years, and it is possible to determine the approximate age of
a writing by the style and form of the language.

1B. Aramaic

1C. INTRODUCTION

The Aramaic of Daniel originated from the ancient West
Semitic language. This language later developed into different
dialects, including Western Aramaic (found in Jerusalem) and
Eastern Aramaic (found in Babylon).

2C. CONTENTIONS OF THE RADICAL CRITICS

Driver observes: "The *Aramaic* of Daniel (which is all but
identical with that of Ezra) is a *Western* Aramaic dialect, of the
type spoken in and about *Palestine*. It is nearly allied to the
Aramaic of the Targums of Onkelos and Jonathan; and still
more so to the Aramaic dialects spoken E. and S.E. of Palestine,
in Palmyra and Nabataea, and known from inscriptions dating
from the 3rd cent. B.C. to the 2nd cent. A.D." 12/471

Driver says the difference ". . . constitutes an argument
against the opinion that the Aramaic of Daniel was that spoken
at Babylon" in the sixth century B.C. 12/473

3C. EVALUATING CRITICAL CONTENTIONS

1D. Contentions

1E. The Aramaic of Daniel is a Western Aramaic dialect.

2E. The Aramaic of Daniel is nearly allied to the Aramaic of
certain Targums dating from the second century B.C.

3E. The Aramaic of Daniel is even more closely allied to the Aramaic dialects spoken east and southeast of Palestine.

4E. This Western Aramaic dialect is known from inscriptions dating from the third century B.C. to the second century A.D.

5E. The Aramaic of Daniel was not spoken in Babylon in the sixth century B.C.

2D. Deduction: Since the Aramaic of Daniel is of the dialect spoken in Palestine in the second century B.C., the book must have been written in the second century B.C.

4C. QUESTIONS IN DISPUTE

1D. Does the Aramaic of Daniel coincide with that used during the second century B.C. in Palestine?

2D. Is it true that the Aramaic of Daniel differs from the Aramaic spoken in Babylon in the sixth century B.C., when conservative scholars claim Daniel was written?

3D. What Aramaic dialect actually is found in Daniel?

5C. ANSWERS

1D. Definition of Aramaic Dialects

Professor Harrison gives a detailed account of the Aramaic in Daniel: "In 1891 S. R. Driver could write quite confidently that the Persian words in Daniel presupposed a period of composition after the Persian empire had been well established; the Greek words demanded, the Hebrew supported, and the Aramaic permitted a date subsequent to the conquest of Palestine by Alexander the Great in 332 B.C. This aphorism was widely quoted by English writers in succeeding decades, and as far as the Aramaic sections were concerned, H. H. Rowley sought to substantiate the assertions of Driver by means of several publications and articles. However, subsequent discoveries and studies have shown the dangers inherent in appealing to the presence of Aramaic elements as incontrovertible evidence for a late date of composition. The term 'Aramaic' is actually of a rather general order, and is employed to describe a group of Semitic dialects closely related to Hebrew and even more closely related to one another. Of the four groups established by linguistic research, namely Old Aramaic, Official Aramaic, Levantine Aramaic, and Eastern Aramaic, the first constituted the language of north-Syrian inscriptions dating from the tenth to the eighth century B.C., where Official

Aramaic also took its roots. This latter was already being employed in governmental offices during the Assyrian period (*ca.* 1100-605 B.C.), and in the succeeding Persian period it was clearly the *lingua franca* of diplomacy and other areas of human activity, even though the Persian monarchs employed a system of cuneiform signs in which to carve royal inscriptions in their own Old Persian language. Aramaic 'dockets' were already becoming attached to cuneiform tablets in Assyrian times, the purpose being to furnish a brief indication of names and dates connected with the tablet, as well as a summary of its contents. Official Aramaic was still in use on 'dockets' throughout the Hellenistic period (330-30 B.C.), as well as on coins, on papyri, and ostraca from Egypt, on Mesopotamian and Egyptian inscriptions, and in some bilingual inscriptions from Asia Minor. Levantine Aramaic appears to have arisen with the early Aramean nomads who penetrated Syria and Palestine, and despite the widespread use of Greek during the Hellenistic period Levantine Aramaic was still the popularly spoken language in New Testament times. Eastern Aramaic originated with the nomadic Arameans who invaded the Tigris-Euphrates region, and some of the dialects survived until Muslim times. As far as the Biblical record is concerned, the antiquity of Aramaic as a spoken language in dialect form can be seen in the use by Laban in Genesis 31:47 of the Aramaic designation Jegar-sahadutha of the cairn that Jacob described by the Hebrew form Galeed or 'witness-heap.' Again, as Young has pointed out, certain Aramaisms that were commonly regarded as late in form have been demonstrated in the Ras Shamra texts of the Amarna Age, and have been seen to include specific ones occurring in Daniel." 19/1124,1125

Note: The Eastern Aramaic mentioned by Harrison does not correspond with the Eastern of Driver. Rather, the Official Aramaic of Harrison is similar to Driver's Eastern.

2D. Daniel Recopied Later and Modernized

Joseph Wilson comments: "Professor Cobern very vigorously asserts that all great living Aramaic scholars are a unit in declaring that the Aramaic of Daniel was never spoken in Babylon. The great living Aramaic scholars mean, of course, that the Aramaic of the text recently discovered and now undergoing decipherment differs somewhat from the Aramaic in which Ezra edited Daniel. This is very likely. Ezra, though brought up in Babylon, had removed to Judea and had caught the dialect of his associates in Jerusalem;

still, some traces of the Babylonian style appear when he transcribes the Aramaic of Daniel. Ezra's Aramaic in his own book differs slightly from his Aramaic when editing Daniel, just as Professor Cobern's English would differ from his English were he editing an English writer of one hundred years ago." 43/64,65

Wilson also says: "As to the Aramaic of Daniel, Canon Driver says 'it is all but identical with that of Ezra.' Precisely what we should expect, for Ezra was born and brought up in Babylon, and, moreover, he and his colleagues edited Daniel. And if Ezra's Aramaic suffered modification at the hands of the subsequent scribes, so would Daniel's." 43/63,64

John H. Raven concludes that even if the Aramaic of Daniel could be proven to be of the Western form, it does not necessarily mean Daniel was composed in Palestine. The book probably was recopied later in Palestine to conform to the common dialect. 32/326

3D. Foreign Words Indicate Sixth Century B.C.

Boutflower believes that by comparing the foreign influences found in the Aramaic of Daniel with those in Aramaic documents which have known dates of composition, the date and place of Daniel's authorship can be determined.

He states: "The Zakir inscription of 850 B.C. has no foreign elements, except perhaps Hebrew. The Sendsherli inscriptions of the latter part of the eighth century B.C. have Assyrian ingredients. The Egypto-Aramaic of the fifth century B.C. has Persian, Babylonian, Hebrew, and Egyptian terms, and perhaps one Latin and three Greek words. The Nabatean has Arabic in large measure, one Babylonian, and a few Greek ones. The Palmyrene has Greek predominantly, some Arabic, and two Sassanian or late Persian words. The Targum of Onkelos has mainly Greek words, five Persian words, and some Hebrew and Babylonian elements. The Targum of Jonathan has yet more Greek nouns and three verbs likewise, Aramaic in form, derived from Greek nouns, at least one Latin word, apparently no Persian words, and only one Babylonian word or form, except such as are found in the Scriptures, and a considerable number of Hebrew words. The Syriac (Edessene) has hundreds of Greek words, a considerable number of which are verbalised; a little Sanskrit, and in later works many Arabic nouns, especially names of persons and places. In New Syriac the foreign elements are predominantly Turkish, Arabic, and Kurdish loan-words.

"Therefore, it being thus apparent that on the basis of foreign elements inbedded in Aramaic dialects, it is possible for the scholar to fix approximately the time and the locality in which the different dialects were spoken; all the more when, as has been shown in the case of Daniel, such a date and locality are required by the vocabulary of the pure Aramaic substratum and favoured, or at least permitted, by its grammatical forms and structure, we are abundantly justified in concluding that the dialect of Daniel, containing as it does so many Persian, Hebrew, and Babylonian elements, and so few Greek words, with not one Egyptian, Latin, or Arabic word, and being so nearly allied in grammatical form and structure to the older Aramaic dialects and in its conglomerate vocabulary to the dialects of Ezra and Egypto-Aramaic, must have been used at or near Babylon at a time not long after the founding of the Persian empire." 4/256,257

Boutflower also notes that "it is deserving of notice that the Book of Daniel contains several Assyro-Babylonian words, such as might be expected in a book written at or near Babylon in the latter half of the sixth century B.C. Further, all the proper names in this Book are found in the Assyro-Babylonian or admit of a derivation from that source, the Hebrew names only excepted: a feature which hardly agrees with the hypothesis that it was written in the age of Antiochus Epiphanes." 4/256

4D. Aramaic of Daniel Not Western

Many scholars hold that the Aramaic of Daniel antedates the period when the language developed distinct Eastern and Western forms.

R. K. Harrison says: "More recent studies in Biblical Aramaic have cast grave doubts upon the advisability of distinguishing sharply between eastern and western branches of the linguistic group, as older scholars were wont to do, thus seriously weakening the force of the assertion by Driver." 19/1125

Stephen M. Clinton asserts that the Aramaic of Daniel antedates these distinctions and, therefore, is neither Eastern nor Western. In addition, the book shows traces of having the Eastern variations removed. These traces could exist only if the older Aramaic had been used originally. 9/39

Thomson points out: "The most prominent trace of this which we see is the form of the imperfect in *L* as *lhva* for the third person singular." 40/xxiii

Thomson finds more Eastern variations by working backward from the Septuagint text. He believes this evidence demands an early date for Daniel's original composition.

Kitchen, professor in the School of Archaeology and Oriental Studies at the University of Liverpool, also states: "Words found in other early West Semitic texts as well as in the Aramaic of Daniel are to be taken as being not merely early Aramaic but as common, early West Semitic, not even peculiar to Aramaic." 47/33

On the other hand, some scholars hold that the Aramaic of Daniel is of the Eastern variety. E. Y. Kutscher, who introduced linguistics into the study of Hebrew and Aramaic, states: "With regard to Biblical Aramaic, which in word order and other traits is of the Eastern type (i.e., freer and more flexible in word order) and has scarcely any Western characteristics at all, it is plausible to conclude that it originated in the East. A final verdict on this matter, however, must await the publication of all the Aramaic texts from Qumran." 3/389

John H. Raven says many scholars are sure that Daniel was written in Eastern Aramaic. The few variations from the normal Eastern Aramaic are explained by the fact that Daniel was an exile from Palestine. 32/326

5D. Aramaic of Daniel Is Old

Rosenthal's studies have shown that Daniel used a form of Aramaic that originated in the courts and governments of the seventh century B.C. This form later spread throughout the Near East. As a result, Harrison points out that the Aramaic of Daniel ". . . cannot be employed as evidence for a late date of the book, and in fact it constitutes a strong argument for a sixth-century B.C. period of composition." 19/1125

E. J. Young states that, as Baumgartner and others have shown, the Aramaic portions in Daniel contain many old grammatical forms. The Ras esh-Shamra texts, discovered in 1929 and written in the 15th century B.C., contain Aramaic elements similar to the Aramaic of Daniel. For instance, Daniel and the texts spell some words with "d" instead of "z" (e.g., dehav for zehav, "gold"). Before the discovery of the Ras esh-Shamra texts, the critics cited these spellings as proof of Daniel's late date. 50/362

Archer asserts: "Recent discoveries of fifth century Aramaic documents, however, have shown quite conclusively that Daniel was, like Ezra, written in a form of Imperial Aramaic

(Reichsaramaisch), an official or literary dialect which had currency in all parts of the Near East." 3/376

Harrison asserts: "The Aramaic sections of Daniel (2:4b-7:28) are by nature closely akin to the language of the fifth-century B.C. Elephantine papyri." 19/1125

Archer claims that another proof for Daniel's early dates is "the fairly frequent internal-vowel change passives." He says that "instead of adhering exclusively to the standard method of expressing the passive (by the prefix *hit-* or *'et-*) the Biblical Aramaic used a *hophal* formation (e.g., *hon hat* from n^e*hat*, *hussaq* from s^e*laq*, *hūbad* from *'ªbad* and *hu'al* from *'ªlal*). No such examples of *hophal* forms have as yet been discovered in any of the Aramaic documents published from the Dead Sea caves (some of which, like the Genesis Apocryphon, date from scarcely a century later than the Maccabean wars)." 3/389

6D. Unlike Second Century B.C. Western Aramaic

In reference to the Aramaic sectarian material found in Qumran, Archer states: "Nor is there the slightest resemblance between the Aramaic of the Genesis Apocryphon and the Aramaic chapters of Daniel." 3/378

The Aramaic of Daniel also differs from the Aramaic of the later Targums in that the direct object particle *yāh* or *yah* is found frequently in the Targums and not in Daniel, while in Daniel l^e is used to introduce the direct object.

Kitchen summarizes: "The result is that nine-tenths of the vocabulary is attested in texts of the fifth century B.C. or earlier. The slender one-tenth remaining consists of words so far found only in sources later than the fifth century B.C. (e.g. Nabataean, Palmyrene or later Aramaic dialects), or so far not attested externally at all." 47/32

Kitchen concludes from the latest evidence: "Where nine-tenths of the vocabulary is clearly old-established (fifth century B.C. and earlier), it is a fair assumption that the lack of attestation of the odd tenth represents nothing more than the gaps in our present knowledge — gaps liable to be filled by new material in the course of time.

"Hence, as far as the main (i.e. Semitic) vocabulary is concerned, we have no warrant whatever to draw any conclusion about the date of Daniel from its Aramaic except to say that any date from the sixth century B.C. onward is possible." 47/34

After a detailed linguistic analysis of the *Genesis Apocryphon*, Archer concludes that it "furnishes very powerful evidence

that the Aramaic of Daniel comes from a considerably earlier
period than the second century B.C. The fact that Targumic
and Talmudic words abound in this first-century document
indicates a considerable interval in time between its
composition and that of Ezra and Daniel. Its use of normal
Semitic word order in the clause as over against Daniel's
tendency to follow a policy of placing the verb late in the
clause points to a definite difference either in geographic
origin (which would eliminate the possibility of Daniel's
Maccabean composition in Palestine) or in epoch. Either
inference is fatal to the pseudepigraph theory. It is fair to say,
therefore, that the overall testimony of this scroll leads to
abandonment of a long-cherished position of higher
criticism, and makes the genuineness of Danielic authorship
of Daniel an even more attractive option than it was before."
87/169

7D. Language Not a Proper Criteria

Kitchen explains that for two or three generations, modern
scholars, such as S. R. Driver, R. D. Wilson, G. R. Driver, W.
Baumgartner, H. H. Rowley, J. A. Montgomery, H. H.
Schaeder and F. Rosenthal, have studied closely the Aramaic
of Daniel. Today their conclusions need revision because of
additional inscriptional material presenting new facts. The
Brooklyn and Borchardt-Driver documents and the Aramaic
documents from Qumran and other cave sites are a few
examples. 47/31,32

In reference to Driver, Charles Boutflower maintains: "Before
his lamented death this dictum, or at any rate the latter part
of it respecting the Aramaic, was considerably modified by
its author, owing to a remarkable discovery [i.e., the
Elephantine papryi]. . . .

"In his letter to The Guardian of November 6, 1907, Prof.
Driver admits that the Aramaic spoken in Egypt in 408 B.C.
'bears many points of resemblance to that found in the Old
Testament — in Ezra, Daniel, and Jer. x.11.' " 4/226

D. J. Wiseman summarizes the findings: "What, then, shall
we say of the Aramaic of Daniel? It is, in itself, as long and
generally agreed, integrally a part of that Imperial Aramaic
which gathered impetus from at least the seventh century
B.C. and was in full use until c. 300 B.C., thereafter falling
away or fossilizing where it was not native and developing
new forms and usages where it was the spoken tongue. If
proper allowance be made for attested scribal usage in the
Biblical Near East (including orthographical and
morphological change, both official and unofficial), then

there is nothing to decide the date of composition of the Aramaic of Daniel *on the grounds of Aramaic* anywhere between the late sixth and the second century B.C. Some points hint at an early (especially pre-300), not late, date — but in large part could be argued to be survivals till the second century B.C., just as third-second century spellings or grammatical forms must be proved to be original to the composition of the work before a sixth-fifth century date could be excluded. The date of the book of Daniel, in short, cannot be decided upon linguistic grounds alone. It is equally obscurantist to exclude dogmatically a sixth-fifth (or fourth) century date on the one hand, or to hold such a date as mechanically proven on the other, *as far as the Aramaic is concerned."* 47/79

E. J. Young states that "it is becoming more and more clear that the languages cannot be employed as arguments against the antiquity of the book." 50/362,363

6C. SUMMARY

Charles Boutflower states: "In concluding this short and imperfect sketch of the Aramaic of the Book of Daniel, instead of Dr. Driver's verdict — *'the Aramaic permits a date after the conquest of Palestine by Alexander the Great'* — I would suggest the following: 'That in view of the evidence furnished, more especially by the Elephantine papyri, as well as by other documents, *the Aramaic permits a date as early as the closing years of the prophet Daniel.'* " 4/240

2B. Persian Words

1C. INTRODUCTION

Present in the Hebrew and particularly in the Aramaic of Daniel are several Persian loan words. The radical critics assume Daniel could not have used the Persian words attributed to him in the Book of Daniel. They say the Persian language did not penetrate the Aramaic of Babylon until long after Cyrus' conquest.

2C. CONTENTIONS OF THE RADICAL CRITICS

Driver professes: "The number of *Persian* words in the Book (especially in the Aramaic part) is remarkable. That such words should be found in books written after the Persian empire was organised, and when Persian influences prevailed, is not more than would be expected; several occur in Ezr. Neh. Est. Chr., and many were permanently naturalised in Aramaic (both Syriac and the Aramaic of the Targums); but that they should be used as a matter of course by Daniel under the Babylonian supremacy, or in the description of Babylonian institutions *before* the conquest of Cyrus, is surprising." 12/464,465

Some of the Persian words, concludes Driver, "are used exactly as in the later Aramaic, and are of a kind that would not be borrowed by one people from another unless intercourse between them had subsisted for a considerable time." 12/470

3C. EVALUATING CRITICAL CONTENTIONS

1D. Observation: A number of Persian words are found in Daniel, most prominently in the Aramaic section.

2D. Assumption: The Book of Daniel asserts that Daniel wrote part of his book before the Persian conquest.

3D. Claim: It is surprising that Daniel, supposedly writing before the Persian conquest, should use Persian words to describe Babylonian institutions.

4D. Assumption: Words from another language are not borrowed freely unless the ethnic groups using distinct languages have had social contact and intercourse for a sufficiently long amount of time.

5D. Contention: The Persian language would not have been familiar enough to an individual of the sixth century B.C. in Babylon for him to utilize Persian words.

6D. Deduction: Therefore, the Book of Daniel must have been written some time later than the sixth century B.C., when sufficient time had elapsed for Aramaic to incorporate certain Persian words.

4C. ANSWERS

1D. Daniel Written During Persian Era

It is a false assumption that conservative scholars hold to the position that Daniel was composed in its final form before the Persians established authority over Babylon. The text is clear that Daniel lived for at least several years under Persian rule. It seems natural that he would incorporate Persian terms in the final writing and editing, especially terms referring to the areas of government and administration. By 530 B.C. the Aramaic spoken in Babylon had been permeated by Persian terms.

Stephen M. Clinton adds: "Daniel lived part of his life under Persian rule. He may have re-edited the early chapters himself including up to date terminology at these points. Most of these words concern government and administration and it would be fitting for Daniel to bring these more in line with the current situation." 9/38

Kitchen writes that ". . . if a putative Daniel in Babylon under the Persians (and who had briefly served them) were to write a book some time after the third year of Cyrus (Dn. 10:1), then a series of Persian words is no surprise. Such a person in the position of close contact with Persian administration that is accorded to him in the book would have to acquire — and use in his Aramaic — many terms and words from his new Persian colleagues (just like the Elamite scribes of Persepolis) from the conquest by Cyrus onwards." 47/41,42

In reference to the absence of Persian loan words from other documents of Daniel's time, Raven points out that several of the words are political in nature and would not appear in contract tablets. As for the other words, not enough information on the language of Nebuchadnezzar's time is available to deny the possibility of Persian influence. Also, this influence would have affected the courts before it affected the people at large. 32/324

"Satrap" is one Persian word which the critics say Daniel could not have written. E. J. Young states: "The Persian title 'satrap' is said to be used in Daniel (e.g., 3:3) as though it were a Babylonian title. But in reply it may be said that this is not necessarily an anachronism. For one thing, it is quite possible that such a term, due to Persian influence, might have been employed in Babylon even during the reign of Nebuchadnezzar. But it is not necessary to make such an assumption. If Daniel wrote after the fall of Babylon, say in the third year of Cyrus, he might very well have employed Persian terms in certain cases as substitutes for the older Babylonian terms. Thus his writing would become understandable to readers who lived during the Persian age. If this were the case the use of the term 'satrap' is in no sense an anachronism." 50/360

Thus, the problem becomes whether Persian words were sufficiently familiar to a sixth century writer in Babylon.

2D.   Early Contact of Aramaic with Old Persian

The following chart was developed by Boutflower:

"To show the wide diffusion of the Arameans, and their contact with Median tribes speaking the Old Persian some 200 years before the probable date of the Book of Daniel.

1650 B.C. Agum-kakrimi, king of Babylon, styles himself 'king of Padan and of Alman' (= Arman, cf. Padan-Aram: Gen. xxviii.2)

1350 B.C. Pudi-ilu, king of Assyria, conquers the Akhlami, an Aramean tribe.

1150 B.C. Ashur-rish-ishi overthrows 'the wide-spread host of the Akhlami.'

1120 B.C. Tiglathpileser I. speaks of 'the Aramean Akhlami the foes of Ashur' as extending from the country of the Shuhites to Carchemish.

1050 B.C. Saul fights against the Aramean 'kings of Zobah': 1 Sam. xiv.47.

1010 B.C. David smites the Arameans of Syria, Damascus, and Aram-naharaim: 2 Sam. viii.3-5, and Ps. lx. title.

885-860 B.C. Ashurnatsirpal conquers Bit Adini (cf. 2 Kings xix.12) and other Aramean states on the Middle Euphrates.

850 B.C. Aramaic inscription of Zakir king of Hamath.

770-730 B.C. Aramaic inscriptions of the kings of Samahla on the E. slope of Amanus, and a little N. of the N.E. angle of the Mediterranean.

745 B.C. Tiglathpileser III. speaks of 'the land of the Arameans' as extending from the Tigris to where the Uknu (the river of Shushan) falls into the Persian Gulf, and mentions Aramean tribes conquered by him whose territories extended to the Median border.

744 B.C. Tiglathpileser transports 65,000 Medes and Arameans to other parts of the empire.

722 B.C. Sargon places captive Israelites among the Arameans on the Khabur, and in 'the cities of the Medes': 2 Kings xvii.6.

536 B.C. The Aramaic of Daniel, interspersed with twenty Old Persian words.

471-411 B.C. The Jews of Elephantine write in Aramaic closely resembling the Aramaic of the Book of Daniel." 4/xvi-xvii

Thus, the Aramaic language had ample opportunity to absorb Persian words before the time of Daniel. Kitchen says that "the almost unconscious assumption that Persian words would take some time to penetrate into Aramaic (i.e., well after 539 B.C.) is erroneous." 47/41

If the Book of Daniel was written in the sixth century B.C., and if adequate opportunities existed for Persian words to infiltrate the Aramaic language, then we might expect to find:

1. Certain Persian words in Daniel.

2. Some of those words in Targums based on Daniel.

3. Similar Persian words in other source documents of the same period.

3D. Persian Words in Daniel No Sign of Late Origin

After comparing the Persian vocabulary of Daniel with that of the Targums, Rowley concludes that the biblical Aramaic is much closer to the Targums (200 B.C.).

Kitchen questions these findings on the following grounds:

1. Twenty-one words is too small a base upon which to build statistical arguments. Rowley himself recognizes this deficiency: "While in literature so scanty as our texts, all arguments on vocabulary are liable to be precarious. . . ." 30/36

2. Rowley compares only the Persian vocabularies of biblical Aramaic and the Targums. He also should have compared the Persian vocabularies of Daniel and the sixth-fifth century B.C. Aramaic documents. If he had done this, he would have found that Daniel contains eight or nine Persian words attested in Official Aramaic contemporary sources. These words support a sixth-fifth century B.C. date as much as the 13 words found in the Targums support a second century B.C. date. 47/36,37

    Kitchen adds: "It should also be remembered that survival of words from Daniel or Ezra in the Targums is to be expected *a priori* — after all, they belong to *one* literary tradition, Jewish, biblical and commentary/interpretation therefor!" 47/42

In 1929, Rowley pointed out that the Aramaic of Daniel had only two Persian words in common with the Aramaic of the fifth century B.C. papyri from Egypt (consisting of 87 documents collected by A. E. Cowley). Rowley used this as evidence for Daniel's late date.

Since then, however, new discoveries have weakened Rowley's theories. Of particular interest are the fifth century B.C. Aramaic documents published by G. R. Driver in 1954 and 1957. These documents contain 26 Persian words, 19 of which occur nowhere else. Three words are found only in the Talmud, and five words are found only in other fifth century B.C. records. No one would use these statistics to show that G. R. Driver's documents were written midway between the fifth and second centuries B.C., as S. R. Driver earlier had done with Daniel. Daniel is statistically close to these documents, having 21 Persian words, seven of which recur only in the Targums, and eight or nine of which recur only in sixth century B.C. sources.

In 1953, E. G. Kraeling also published new documents. In

this group, half of the Persian words are not found in any other contemporary records. 47/38,39

In reference to the new discoveries, Kitchen concludes that:

1. "Statistics are virtually worthless" because the documents have few Persian words.

2. The few Persian words common to Daniel and Ezra and Cowley's 87 papyri "prove *only* that our knowledge of the total impact of Old Persian upon Imperial Aramaic (and its continuations) is grossly inadequate."

3. Daniel has several more Persian words in common with fifth century B.C. documents than Rowley allowed in 1929.

4. Persian words in Daniel found in both sixth-fifth century B.C. and late (Targumic/Talmudic) sources only proves that they were used for a long time in Aramaic. Words in Daniel found only in late sources are matched by other words found only in early sources. Daniel's date of composition cannot be determined by this criteria. 47/39,40

4D. Persian Words in Daniel of Early Origin

There is positive evidence in the Old Greek and later translations of Daniel that the Persian words in the book could not have originated in the second century B.C. In Daniel 3:2,3, the Persian words for satraps, prefects and governors are translated fairly accurately. But the translators guessed badly on the meanings for counselors, treasurers, law officers and magistrates. Why do they translate some of the words right and some of them wrong?

Obviously, the meanings of some of the words had been forgotten or changed by the time the translators did their work.

The first Greek translation of Daniel was written around 100 B.C. at the latest. If Daniel were written around 165 B.C., it seems incredible that the Persian words would have lost or changed their meaning in so short a time (by Near Eastern standards). Therefore, the date of composition must be much earlier, probably within memory of the Persian rule (*i.e.*, between 539 and 280 B.C., allowing a 50-year lapse after the Persian empire fell). 47/42,43

Kitchen points out that "the Persian words in Daniel are specifically *Old Persian* words." Also, when Persian words in Daniel do not correspond with known Old

Persian words, they can be compared with reconstructable forms in Old Persian, but not with later forms. Since Old Persian gave way to Middle Persian around 300 B.C., Daniel's Aramaic must be from an era before Persia fell to the Greeks because it does not include any Middle Persian expressions. 47/43

Donald J. Wiseman remarks, therefore, that the Persian loan words in Daniel suggest an origin before 300 B.C. The author of Daniel could not have borrowed these words after that date, but would have used Middle Persian words. This supports an early date for Daniel's composition. 47/77

5C. SUMMARY

We have shown that Daniel probably wrote his book after Cyrus' conquest and that Persian words could have penetrated the Aramaic language by this time. The Maccabean theory of authorship would demand that the Persian words be of late derivation, but in actuality they reveal an early origin.

Charles Boutflower claims that the Persian words ". . . must, indeed, no longer be regarded as stumbling-blocks in our path, but rather as strong confirmations of the orthodox view that the Book of Daniel was written within and towards the close of the times which it describes, and that Daniel himself was the writer." 4/241

3B. Greek Words

1C. THE PROBLEM

Daniel 3:5 (within the Aramaic section) contains three words of Greek origin. The radical critics believe that Greek could not have entered the Aramaic language until the time of Alexander's conquest.

One of the three Greek loan words is *qayterōs*, translated in the Septuagint as *kithara*. However, some believe that *kithara* may be a foreign loan word to the Greek language. This would mean that both *qayterōs* and *kithara* are derived from a common unknown ancestor. In any case, the word probably denotes a kind of lyre, although this has not yet been completely proved. 47/24

The other two words are *psantērîn* and *sûmpōn^eya*. Although neither word is attested in Greek until after the sixth century B.C., this does not mean that they did not exist in Daniel's time. *Sumphōnia* was used by Pythagoras apparently around 530 B.C. Pindar used *sumphōnos* in his first Pythian ode, *c.* 470 B.C. *Sumphōnia* cannot be attested as the name of a specific musical instrument or an orchestra until the time of Polybius (second century B.C.).

In all probability, as we shall see, they were introduced to Babylon by Greek traders, mercenaries or captives before the rise of the Persian empire.

Gleason Archer says it is significant that all three Greek words are names for musical instruments. Such names often are borrowed as the instruments become known. For example, the English language has borrowed the Italian words "piano" and "viola." 3/375

Some critics also assign two or three other words to Greek origin, but Archer shows that this has been proved incorrect. Two of the words, *kārōz* and *pathgām*, are derived from Old Persian. 3/375

2C. CONTENTIONS OF THE RADICAL CRITICS

Driver says: "Whatever may be the case with *kītharos*, it is incredible that *psantērîn* and *sumpōnyāh* can have reached Babylon *c.* 550 B.C. Any one who has studied Greek history knows what the condition of the Greek world was in that century, and is aware that the arts and inventions of civilised life streamed then into Greece from the East, not from Greece eastwards. Still, if the instruments named were of a primitive kind, such as the *kītharos* (in Homer), it is *just* possible that it might be an exception to the rule, and that the Babylonians might have been indebted for their knowledge of it to the Greeks; so that, had *qayterōs* stood alone, it could not, perhaps, have been pressed. But no such exception can be made in the case of *psantērîn* and *sumpōnyāh*." 12/470,471

Driver concludes: ". . . 'the Greek words *demand* . . . a date *after the conquest of Palestine by Alexander the Great* (B.C. 332).' " 12/476

3C. EVALUATING CRITICAL CONTENTIONS

1D. Historical observation: Alexander the Great did not conquer Palestine and the nations surrounding it until about 332 B.C.

2D. Historical Claims

1E. The Greeks possessed primitive musical instruments.

2E. The Greek words *psantērîn* and *sûmpōn^eyâ* do not describe primitive instruments.

3E.   Civilized arts and inventions streamed from the East into Greece, not from Greece eastwards.

3D. Contentions

1E.   The Greeks would not have had such instruments in the sixth century B.C.; hence, they could not have had Greek names.

2E.   The Greeks would not have used such words until after the conquests of Alexander the Great.

3E.   These Greek words would not have been available to a writer in Babylon in the sixth century B.C.

4C. ANSWERS

1D.   Absence of Greek Words Gives Evidence of Early Composition

Actually, the presence of only three Greek musical terms is one of the strongest evidences against Daniel's composition in the second century B.C. The Aramaic of Daniel easily borrowed foreign expressions. About 20 Persian words are used, almost all of which are governmental terms. Since by 170 B.C. a Greek-speaking government had controlled Palestine for 160 years, it is remarkable, if Daniel were written in the second century B.C., that no more than three Greek words are found in the book. Especially remarkable is the absence of governmental terms. The Books of Maccabees reveal that Greek culture and customs had deeply influenced Jewish society at this time. This absence of Greek words implies that the language of Daniel dates before the Greek period. 3/375

Boutflower declares that "there are only three Greek words to match some twenty Persian, and that had the Book been written in the time of Antiochus Epiphanes, more than a century and a half after the conquests of Alexander, having regard to the wonderful Hellenising of Western Asia caused by those conquests, we should certainly have expected to find more Greek words than Persian. *It is the fewness of the Greek words, coupled with the fact that they are only the names of musical instruments, that must prove fatal to the critics' theory that the Book was written in 165 B.C.;* fatal, also, to Prof. Driver's dictum, 'the Greek words *demand* a date *after the conquest of Palestine by Alexander the Great.'* Such a demand I utterly fail to see." 4/246

Kitchen agrees, referring to the lack of Greek words
compared to the number of Persian words. He points out
that in the literature of the ancient Near East, the writer
usually describes an earlier period with terms of his own
time. Thus, if Daniel were written in 165 B.C., far into the
Greek period, then one would expect Aramaic and
Hebrew sections describing the Persian regime to be
dotted with Greek terms. This is not the case; rather, some
20 Persian words are used, some to describe the previous
Babylonian empire, as one would expect if the book was
written in the sixth century B.C.

2D.   Early Greek Influence

Contrary to what Driver believes, there is ample evidence
of early Greek influence on the Near East.

Mitchell and Joyce compiled the following chart of Greek
contact with the Near East:

Eighth century B.C. Greek pottery in Syria, even Nineveh
750 B.C. Greek pottery in Palestine
Seventh century B.C. Greek supreme imports
    predominant at Al Mina; Greek pottery in Syria,
    Phoenicia and Babylon
660 B.C. Greek bronze shield at battle site of Carchemish
605-585 B.C. Greek mercenaries serve in Babylonian
    forces
595-570 B.C. Greek artisans employed in Babylon by
    Nebuchadnezzar
590 B.C. Greek mercenaries of Psammetichus II leave
    names in Nubia
Sixth-fifth century B.C. Greek settlement at Minet el
    Beida (near Ugarit)
Fifth century B.C. Greek pottery in Syria and Palestine
    down to Gulf of Aqaba 47/44-46

Boutflower developed the following chart:

*"To show the contact of Assyria, Babylonia, and Egypt with
    the Asiatic Greeks for over a century before the age of
    Daniel.*

715 B.C. Sargon clears the E. Levant of Greek pirates:
    Cylinder Inscr., line 21.
711 B.C. A Greek king in Ashdod: *Khorsabad Inscr.*, line
    95.
707 B.C. Seven kings of Cyprus send presents to Sargon at
    Babylon: *Ibid.* line 196.
698 B.C. Sennacherib, to keep open the trade route,
    encounters the Greeks in Cilicia, and builds an

'Athenian temple' at Tarsus: *Cuneiform Texts from Babylonian Tablets in the Br. Museum*, pt. xxvi.

697 B.C. Sennacherib employs Greek captives to build him a fleet on the Tigris: *Bull Inscr.*, No. 4, lines 56-60.

674 B.C. Ten kings of Cyprus — nine of them with Greek names — send materials to build Esarhaddon's palace at Nineveh: *Esarhaddon, Cylinder B*, col. 5, lines 19-27.

664 B.C. Greeks help Psammetichus I. of Egypt to conquer the Dodekarchy. In return he uses Greek mercenaries, and plants two camps of them at Daphnae on either side of the Pelusiac branch of the Nile: *Herod.* bk.ii. 152,154.

605 B.C. Nebuchadnezzar, after his campaign against Egypt, plants colonies in Babylonia, consisting of Jews, Phonicians, Syrians, and 'of the nations belonging to Egypt': *Joseph. c. Apion*, bk.i. 19.

595 B.C. Nebuchadnezzar, rebuilding the Old Palace at Babylon, employs Greek architectural decorations on the facade of the throne-room: *Koldewey's Excavations*, pp. 104,105, and plate opposite p. 130.

587 B.C. In the 18th year of Nebuchadnezzar (according to the LXX.), three instruments with Greek names are found in the king's band amongst 'all kinds of music': Dan. iii. 5." 4/xvii,xviii

Mitchell and Joyce state: "One significant fact is the apparent wide distribution, especially in the first millennium B.C., of particular types of instruments, for in many cases the instruments on those isolated islands of evidence we have — the Assyrian reliefs, the Neo-Hittite monuments and the Greek vase paintings — are surprisingly similar. It seems from this that the transfer of musical instruments, perhaps through the agency of musicians' guilds, may have been taking place over long distances." 47/22

Archer states: ". . . as early as the reign of Sargon (722-705 B.C.) there were, according to the Assyrian records, Greek captives who were sold into slavery from Cyprus, Ionia, Lydia and Cilicia. The Greek poet Alcaeus of Lesbos (fl. 600 B.C.) mentions that his brother Antimenidas served in the Assyrian army. It is therefore evident that Greek mercenaries, Greek slaves and Greek musical instruments were current in the Semitic Near East long before the time of Daniel. It is also significant that in the Neo-Babylonian ration tablets published by E. F. Weidner, Ionian carpenters and shipbuilders are mentioned among the recipients of rations from Nebuchadnezzar's commissary — along with musicians from Ashkelon and elsewhere (cf. Jojachin König von Juda in *Mélanges Syriens*, II, 1939, pp. 923-935)." 3/387

Kitchen adds: "In other words, Greek traders were active in the Levant from the days of Amos onwards, and their wares penetrated to Nineveh and Babylon. Greek mercenaries are attested in the Orient from the late seventh century B.C. onwards." 47/45

In addition, Nebuchadnezzar employed Greek artisans to work in Babylon. The Persian empire also made use of Greek artisans. 47/46

Sayce says: "Cuneiform decipherment has made it questionable whether the occurrence of words which may be of Greek origin is equally certain evidence of a late date — There were Greek colonies on the coast of Palestine in the time of Hezekiah — The Tel-el-Amarna tablets have enabled us to carry back a contact between Greece and Canaan to a still earlier period — It is thus possible that there was intercourse and contact between the Canaanites or Hebrews in Palestine and the Greeks of the Aegean as far back as the age of Moses." 35/494,495

Harrison concludes: "The early nature and extent of Greek influence in the entire area can be judged from the presence of Greek colonies in mid-seventh-century B.C. Egypt at Naucratis and Tahpanhes, as well as by the fact that Greek mercenary troops served in both the Egyptian and Babylonian armies at the Battle of Carchemish in 605 B.C." 19/1126

There are even early examples of Greek words in the Aramaic language. The Greek word *statēr* occurs in the Aramaic papyri from Egypt (*c.* 400 B.C.). Thus, Greek expressions had penetrated Imperial Aramaic 100 years before the time of Alexander. 47/46

Kitchen observes: "Greek words occur in Imperial Aramaic at the end of the fifth century B.C. (*statēr*, probably *dōrēma?*, just possibly others), and there is nothing to stop them appearing earlier." 47/77

One of the words in Daniel, *sûmpōn^eyâ*, is possibly a transliteration of a dialectical form of *tympanon*. *Tympanon* dates back to at least the sixth century B.C. The evidence for this view is as follows:

1. In Eastern Greek dialects, it is common to exchange "t" for "s" before "l" and "y."

2. *Tympanon* sometimes is written *typanon*. This may explain why *sipōnya* appears instead of *sûmpōn^eyâ* in Daniel 3:10.

3. The exchange of "o" for "a" in the second syllable is paralleled by Ionic *glassa* for *glōssa*.

4. The *tympanon* was a percussion instrument. At least one percussion instrument probably would have been included in the orchestra.

5. The critics claim *sûmpōneyâ* is derived from *symphonia* and means "bagpipe." But this does not explain why the instrument is separated from the other wind instruments in the list. Another possible explanation is that Daniel uses the word to mean "in unison," which is the meaning of the adjective *symphonous* in *Hymni Homerici, ad Mercurium* 51 (early sixth century B.C.). 47/25,26

R. K. Harrison states: "Furthermore, while the names of the instruments mentioned may appear to be Greek in nature, the instruments themselves are of Mesopotamian origin. The 'harp' can probably be identified, according to Werner, with one of the many Asiatic precursors of the classical Greek *kithara*, and being a strictly secular instrument it fitted quite well into the picture of the banquet of Nebuchadnezzar. The 'psaltery,' also translated 'harp,' was the old dulcimer, the Persian-Arabic *santir*, and its occurrence both on Assyrian reliefs and in eastern Mediterranean culture in the first millennium B.C. generally is amply attested." 19/1126

Mitchell and Joyce summarize: "With such scanty material for any identification of these instruments, it may equally be argued that a sixth-century date for the orchestra cannot be categorically denied." 46/27

3D. Lack of Evidence

The appearance of the three Greek words *qayterōs (kitharis)*, *psanterîn (psalterion)* and *sûmpōneyâ (symphonia)* in Daniel 3 does not mean the book must have been composed after Alexander the Great conquered the Near East. The critics allege that since *sûmpōneyâ* is not found in extant Greek literature until the fourth century, then Daniel must be at least that late. This is a false assumption, however, because we do not possess enough important classical Greek literature on which to base the dating of a word. 3/374

R. Yaron, lecturer in Roman law at the Hebrew University in Jerusalem, points out that if a Greek word appears in an Aramaic document before it appears in actual Greek documents, then earlier Greek documents containing that word have not yet been discovered. Such an occurrence proves only the inadequacy of extant Greek source-material. 48/104

The discovery of the Elephantine papyri has shattered the critics' claim that Greek could not have entered Aramaic during the time of Daniel. B. K. Waltke expresses that "One can no longer echo the dictum that the three Greek words depicting musical instruments in Daniel 3 demand a date after 330 B.C. Greek words are now attested in the Aramaic documents of Elephantine dated to the fifth century B.C. For example, one document refers to a 'stater' as the *KSP JWN*, meaning 'silver of Greece.' Rabinowitz has pointed out an additional three words that are possibly Greek words in the Elephantine papyri." 74/324

5C. SUMMARY

Kitchen writes this summary: "Of the three terms, *qytrs* (*kitharos*) is already known from Homer (i.e., eighth century B.C. at latest), and so has no bearing on date whatever. This leaves only the two words *psntrn* and *smpny'*, commonly stated to be attested only from the second century B.C. or so with the required meanings. On these words, here, suffice it to reiterate that this is only *negative* evidence, i.e. *lack* of evidence, and there is nothing to prevent earlier occurrences from turning up some day in future Greek epigraphic finds. There are plenty of parallels in the Near East for the accidental preservation of words of one language as loan-words in another tongue at an earlier date than extant *known* occurrences in the original tongue. In Mesopotamia we have clay tablets, and in Egypt papyri, ostraca and monumental texts, on a far grander scale of survival than any contemporary records of West Semitic (even with Ugaritic) or classical Greek. No-one raises objections when a West Semitic word (or a particular meaning of a word) turns up as a loan-word in Egyptian New Kingdom texts or in the Mari tablets, perhaps *centuries* before it is attested in any West Semitic inscriptions or papyri, and exactly the same principle should apply to Greek. Thus, these two words *psntrn* and *smpny'* — and *only* two words from an entire book! — are necessarily indecisive, when the only appeal is to ignorance." 47/48,49

Edwin Yamauchi, professor of history at Miami University, Oxford, Ohio, after careful and extended study of the Greek words, concludes: "The only element of surprise to this writer is that there are not more Greek words in such documents." 81/94

4B. Hebrew

1C. INTRODUCTION

The Book of Daniel is written partly in Hebrew. The Hebrew language underwent a great change in style around the time of

Nehemiah. The critics claim that Daniel's style resembles the later Hebrew style; thus the book could not have been written during the time of Nebuchadnezzar and Cyrus.

2C. CONTENTIONS OF THE RADICAL CRITICS

Driver gives the following account of the development of the Hebrew language: "In order properly to estimate the *Hebrew* of Daniel, it must be borne in mind that the great turning-point in Hebrew style falls in the age of *Nehemiah*. The purest and best Hebrew prose style is that of JE and the earlier narratives incorporated in Jud. Sam. Kings: Dt. (though of a different type) is also thoroughly classical: Jer., the *latter* part of Kings, Ezekiel, II Isaiah, Haggai, show (though not all in the same respects or in the same degree) *slight* signs of being later than the writings first mentioned; but in the 'memoirs' of Ezra and Nehemiah (*i.e.* the parts of Ezra and Neh. which are the work of these reformers themselves, see p. 511), and (in a less degree) in the contemporary prophecy of Malachi, a more marked change is beginning to show itself, which is still more palpable in the Chronicles (end of the 4th cent. B.C.), Esther, and Ecclesiastes. The change is visible in both vocabulary and syntax. In vocabulary many new words appear, often of Aramaic origin, occasionally Persian, and frequently such as continued in use afterwards in the 'New-Hebrew' of the Mishnah (200 A.D.), & c.: old words also are sometimes used with new meanings or applications. In syntax, the ease and grace and fluency of the earlier writers (down to at least Zech. 12-14) has passed away; the style is often laboured and inelegant: sentences constantly occur which a pre-exilic, or even an *early* post-exilic, writer would have moulded differently: new and uncouth constructions make their appearance. The three books named do not, however, exhibit these peculiarities in equal proportions: Ecclesiastes (p. 445) has the most striking *Mishnic* idioms: the Chronicler (p. 502 ff.) has many peculiarities of his own, and may be said to show the greatest uncouthness of style; but they agree in the possession of many common (or similar) features, which differentiate them from all previous Hebrew writers (including Zech. Hagg. Mal.), and which recur in them with decidedly greater frequency and prominence than in the memoirs of Ezr. and Neh. And the Hebrew of Daniel is of the type just characterised: in all distinctive features it resembles, not the Hebrew of Ezekiel, or even of Haggai and Zechariah, but that of the age *subsequent to Nehemiah*." 12/473

Driver contends: "The verdict of the language of Daniel is thus clear . . . the Hebrew *supports* . . . a date *after the conquest of Palestine by* Alexander the Great (332 B.C.)." 12/476

3C. EVALUATING CRITICAL CONTENTIONS

  1D. Linguistic Developments

    1E. The Hebrew language underwent certain changes in vocabulary and syntax.

    2E. The turning point in the development of the Hebrew linguistic style occurred during the time of Nehemiah.

  2D. Linguistic claim: The Hebrew section of Daniel is similar in style to this later Hebrew.

  3D. Contention: Since Daniel is written in this later style, it must have been composed when this style was in use, later than the sixth century B.C.

4C. ANSWERS

  1D. Absence of Greek Words

A significant characteristic of the Hebrew portions of Daniel is the total absence of Greek words. In contrast, several Persian terms, such as "palace" (*appenden* in 11:45, from *apadana*), "nobleman" (*part^emin* in 1:3, from *fratama*) and "king's portion" (*patbag* in 1:5, from *patibaga*), are present. By 170 B.C., a Greek-speaking government had controlled Palestine for 160 years, and Greek customs and culture had made deep inroads, as shown in the Books of Maccabees. If Daniel were written around 165 B.C., the absence of Greek terms, especially political and administrative terms, is inexplicable. 3/376

  2D. Daniel's Hebrew Compared to Others'

    1E. Chronicles

The critics point out that the Hebrew of Daniel is crude and late, like the Hebrew of Chronicles, which dates, they say, around 300 B.C. But, if that evaluation is justifiable, one should expect Daniel's Hebrew to be somewhat less polished and literary, since he spent most of his life in a foreign court. In addition, there is no need to date Chronicles later than 400 B.C. Therefore, Chronicles' likeness to Daniel does not mean that Daniel was not the author.

    2E. Ezekiel

Jenkins concludes: "Before leaving the literary argument against the early date of Daniel, it would be well to mention the similarity of the Hebrew to that of the Book of Ezekiel. Like every other Hebrew writer Daniel used freely the language of his time. Although the language is very similar to that of Ezekiel, the style of Daniel is quite different. Pusey reports that Daniel's Hebrew 'is freer from unusual grammatical forms than that of Ezekiel.' In the light of this Daniel could not have been written from Ezekiel. The similarity merely strengthens the argument that they wrote during the same period and used words and idioms peculiar to that time." 21/81

3E. Nehemiah

Stephen Clinton believes that the "fact that the Hebrew of Daniel is similar to the Hebrew of Nehemiah does not reflect a late date. The changes of style in the Hebrew at Jerusalem began just before the time of Nehemiah in Babylon, where Aramaic began to creep in. If Daniel wrote in Babylon, we would expect this influence to show up in his writing." 9/40; 40/xv-xvii

4E. Ecclesiasticus

Gleason Archer refers to the significant differences between the Hebrew of Daniel and the Hebrew of Ecclesiasticus, written by Jesus ben Sirach between 200 and 170 B.C. Israel Levi (*Introduction to the Hebrew Text of Ecclesiasticus*, 1904) lists some of the major differences (pp. xi, xii):

1. New verbal forms borrowed mainly from the Aramaic.

2. Excessive use of the *hiphil* and *hithpael* conjunctions.

3. Peculiarities of various sorts heralding the approach of Mishnaic Hebrew. 3/391

Of the Qumran material, Archer states that "none of the sectarian documents composed in Hebrew ('The Manual of Discipline,' 'The War of the Children of Light Against the Children of Darkness,' 'The Thanksgiving Psalms') in that collection show any distinctive characteristics in common with the Hebrew chapters of Daniel." 3/378

3D. Specific Contested Words

To support his contention, Driver lists about 30 expressions in Daniel which, he says, rarely or never occurred in earlier Hebrew literature. Three of the most significant expressions will be examined.

1E. *Malkut*

Driver states that "the earlier language, in similar sentences (Kings, *passim*), dispenses with *malkut*. 12/506 (1913 edition)

Martin does not understand why Driver includes this word. It "is not restricted to a particular formula," and is not new (*cf.* Numbers 24:7; I Samuel 20:31; Jeremiah 10:7; 49:34; 52:31; Nehemiah 9:35; 12:22; Ezra 1:1; 4:5,6; 7:1; 8:1). "It is not only well attested but it is a pattern of noun widely used in all periods of Hebrew, and is found in Akkadian as early as Hammurabi." 47/28

2E. *Hattāmîd* (the continual burnt offering)

Driver states that this word would not stand by itself if Daniel was written in the sixth century B.C. "(In the older Heb. the full phrase *holat hattāmîd* is always used, Nu. 28, 10&f. Neh. 10,34.)" 12/474

Martin states: "Included in the list is *hattāmîd*, 'the continual burnt offering.' There would seem to be even less justification for including this than some of the other terms. There is ample evidence to show that Hebrew, like many other languages, made wide use of elliptical expressions. In fact, one philologist (W. Havers) has even gone so far as to speak of ellipis as 'a universal human tendency.' " 47/29

An ellipsis is an omission of one or more words from a phrase which does not change the meaning of that phrase. For example, we often say something like "the race he won" instead of "the race *that* he won." In ancient literature, a common example was to say "east" instead of "east wind." In other words the specifying complement takes on the whole meaning of the phrase. In the same way *tāmîd* came to mean continual burnt offering. Originally the Hebrew had a group of phrases containing *ōlat*, which means "offering." Examples are *'ōlat tāmîd*, "continual burnt offering"; *'ōlat halboger*, "morning offering"; *'ōlat sabbāt*, "sabbath offering." For convenience, the *'ōlat* was dropped, and the specifying complement, in this case *hattāmîd*, took on the meaning of the whole phrase. 47/29,30

Martin testifies: "There is abundant evidence to show that such a process was operative in Hebrew. It would indeed have been surprising if such a group as *'ōlat hattāmîd*, 'continual burnt offering,' had remained unaffected." 47/30

3E. *Amar l*

Driver states: "*Amar l* 1,3. 18. 2,2 = *to command to*, . . . where the older language would prefer the *direct*." 12/474

In reference to *amar l*, Martin says: "If this is meant to

imply that this is peculiar to Daniel and late Hebrew, then it would involve postulating a nuance in meaning which would be (virtually) indemonstrable, for the phrase is found in classical Hebrew and, moreover, it occurs in certain passages that must have been familiar to every pious and literate Jew." 47/29

Several examples are found in Deuteronomy 9:25; Joshua 22:33; I Samuel 30:6; and II Samuel 1:18. In each of these cases the word could just as well be read "command" instead of "said," its usual translation. Exodus 2:14 shows that this syntactical pattern was already in existence. A similar pattern is seen in I Kings 5:19 (5:5 in English). The construction is also found in Nehemiah 9:15 and 9:23, and in a sense, it is not distinguishable from Daniel.

5C. SUMMARY

Martin summarizes: "To make out a plausible case for the lateness of Daniel on lexical grounds, one would have to show not only that the words or idioms did not occur earlier, but that there was *prima facie* evidence against the possibility of their appearing. There is no intrinsic probability that any of the terms listed could not have been used much earlier. In fact, one must proceed with the utmost caution in making pronouncements on the extent of a given vocabulary. It is well known that words that are not recorded in the literary language are to be found in the dialects. All that one is justified in saying is that a certain word occurs in the extant documents for the first time. There is nothing about the Hebrew of Daniel that could be considered extraordinary for a bilingual or, perhaps in this case, a trilingual speaker of the language in the sixth century B.C." 47/30

Joseph Wilson concludes: "Professor Cheyne, though one of the most radical critics, shows good sense when he says, 'From the Hebrew of the Book of Daniel no important inference as to its date can be safely drawn.' " 43/63

chapter 5
More Attacks:
The Critics
Support Their Case

5A. ADDITIONAL ARGUMENTS

The following arguments sometimes are presented by the radical critics to support a late date for the Book of Daniel. They do not constitute the main body of alleged evidence, as do the previous arguments, but frequently are used to support the historical and linguistic arguments.

1B. Exegetical Arguments

The following arguments stem from the radical critics' interpretation of the events and prophecies in Daniel and their view of the author's reason for recording them.

1C. INTEREST OF BOOK CULMINATES IN ANTIOCHUS EPIPHANES

1D. Arguments of the Radical Critics

S. R. Driver argues that "it is certainly remarkable that the revelations respecting him [Antiochus Epiphanes] should be given to Daniel, in *Babylon,* nearly four centuries previously . . ." and that "it must be frankly owned that grounds exist which, though not adequate to *demonstrate*, yet make the opinion a *probable* one, that the Book, as we have it, is a work of the age of Antiochus Epiphanes. The interest of the Book manifestly *culminates* in the relations subsisting between the Jews and Antiochus." 12/477

With this in mind, the critics say that the sections dealing with Daniel in the Babylonian and Persian courts are based on reliable traditions. They were written during the days of persecution under Antiochus Epiphanes to encourage the Jews by their example of faithfulness in other troubled times. The critics believe that Antiochus is the "little horn" of chapters seven and eight and that Daniel's prophecies concerning the time beyond his reign are vague. 32/327

2D. Answers

J. D. Wilson asks: "Suppose it true — which it is not — that the prophecies terminate in this vile man; how does that prove that the prophecies were not written at the time the evidence shows them to have been written?" 43/122

Clinton contends: "There remains one detail too irritating to be overlooked. In many of Driver's arguments he uses words such as 'reasonable to suppose,' 'surely,' 'highly improbable,' 'can be understood as,' 'could occur after,' etc. It is one thing to apply these words after detailed explanation has been given to justify them. It is another matter to use such words because one feels sure that if he did give full analysis, the facts would sustain his preconceived ideas. Driver's use of these words in the latter context is a further revelation of his *a priori* philosophical basis." 9/33

"This explanation of the data in Daniel," says Archer, "which is as old as the neo-Platonic polemicist Porphyry (who died in A.D. 303), depends for its validity on the soundness of the premise that there are no accurate predictions fulfilled subsequently to 165 B.C. This proposition, however, cannot successfully be maintained in the light of the internal evidence of the text and its correlation with the known facts of ancient history." 3/396

(Refer to chapter 2, Fulfilled Prophecy, pp. 15-25.)

As Raven explains, the point of view expressed in Daniel provides a key to dating the book: "It is natural that Daniel's predictions in the Exile should give great prominence to the next great affliction of the Jews under a foreign tyrant. Yet the book does not present to us the history of the Exile from the standpoint of the time of Antiochus but the times of Antiochus from the standpoint of the Exile. And prominent as are those times in Daniel's prophetic view, they by no means eclipse what to him was beyond them." 32/328

J. D. Wilson states why these prophecies were justified: "There was coming upon the Jewish people a trial which threatened to extirpate true religion from the earth. There was danger that all the Jews would be swept into Greek idolatry. The danger was real, as is evidenced by the fact that great numbers of them did become thoroughly Hellenized. Greek manners and Greek religion became popular even in Jerusalem. To hold them firm in their ancient faith, they were forewarned; the oppression would not last forever. God was in the heavens watching their actions. He knew all that should befall them, and He tells them particularly and specifically of that crisis in their history. They needed

support for that special time of distress, and that is the time which is sketched so accurately in Dan. xi. There never has been a time since in which the Jews were in danger of letting go their religion. The warning was specific. What its effect was we know. The faithful sons of Abraham stood by their faith and preserved religion. Forewarned was forearmed. Without that prophecy to encourage them it had been madness to enter upon the struggle against the Syrian tyrant. If they had not made that struggle, gross idolatry would have been everywhere triumphant, and not a spot would have been left upon the earth where the one God was worshipped. The occasion justified the prophecy, if justification is needed. But significant and critical as was that occasion, there is more in Daniel than the Syrian oppressor."
43/122-124

In the past, God always had forewarned the Jewish people of coming times of trouble, and always with the perspective of the Jewish nation as His chosen people and with the promise of eventual triumph over the threatening situation. Ultimately, this would culminate in the time of great prosperity and peace for all the earth through God's blessing upon His chosen people.

R. D. Wilson summarizes: "The stupendous crisis justified the prediction; the prediction justified the expectation of deliverance." 45/276

Driver admits the need for these prophecies when he says that "under Antiochus Epiphanes, the very existence of the theocracy was threatened, as it had never been threatened before, by a coalition of heathen foes without with false brethren within. Hence the question *when* the heathen domination would cease was anxiously asked by all faithful Jews. And the answer is given in the Book of Daniel." 12/480

If a Jew could see the need for this in the days of the Maccabees, could not God see the need 400 years earlier and provide for it?

Another reason for the emphasis on Antiochus is that he was to prefigure the final antichrist of the great tribulation. This explains why the prophecy in Daniel 11 accurately relates events in the time of Antiochus until verse 40, and then is seemingly in error. Actually, at this point the figure of Antiochus Epiphanes blends into the figure of the final antichrist.

Dr. Gleason Archer points out: "S. R. Driver admits that these last-mentioned verses do not correspond with what is known of the final stages of Antiochus' career; actually, he

met his end at Tabae in Persia after a vain attempt to plunder
the rich temple of Elymais in Elam." 3/396

Contrary to what the critics say, the focus of Daniel is not
entirely on Antiochus Epiphanes. The prophecy of the 70
weeks (Daniel 9:24-27) goes beyond Antiochus to the time of
Christ and the destruction of Jerusalem by Titus in A.D. 70.
32/329

2C.   DETAIL OF PROPHECIES

1D.   Arguments of the Radical Critics

S. R. Driver assumes that "while down to the period of
Antiochus' persecution the *actual* events are described with
surprising distinctness, after this point *the distinctness ceases*;
the prophecy either breaks off altogether, or merges in an
ideal representation of the Messianic future. Daniel's
perspective, while thus true (approximately) to the period of
Antiochus Epiphanes, is at fault as to the interval which was
actually to follow before the advent of the Messianic age."
12/478

Driver adds: "The minuteness of the predictions, embracing
even special events in the distant future, is also out of
harmony with the analogy of prophecy." 12/478

2D.   Evaluating Critical Contentions

1E.   Daniel's perspective, after describing the period of
Antiochus Epiphanes, is inaccurate in describing the
interval of history between Antiochus and a future
Messianic period.

2E.   The minute detail in Daniel's prophecy conflicts with the
purpose and spirit of prophecy.

3D.   Answers

The irony here is that the critics, disbelievers in prophetic
revelation, set up themselves as arbiters of what a prophecy
may contain. This position, as ridiculous as the attempt to
stand on both sides of a fence, casts grave doubts on any
criteria they propose.

Contrary to Driver's opinion, Daniel's minuteness is not
"out of harmony" with other prophecy in the Old Testament.
Some examples of other detailed prophecies of events far in
the future are: Isaiah 13:19-22; 14:23; 34:6-15; Jeremiah
31:38-40; 47:5; 51:26,43; Ezekiel 25:3,4; 26; 28:22,23; Hosea
13:16; Amos 1:8; Micah 1:6; Nahum 1:8,10; 2:6; 3:10,13,19;
Zephaniah 2:4,6,7.

Also, more than 300 detailed prophecies concerning the Messiah are foretold hundreds of years before their fulfillment in Christ. 71/147-183

The critics claim that the prophecies concerning Antiochus are detailed and clear, while the prophecies concerning the time beyond Antiochus are vague and hidden. This distinction is imagined. The prophecies concerning Antiochus are as "vague" as the rest. The critics admit this by using such words as "probable," "incorrect," author's "ignorance of fact" and obscurity "owing to our ignorance regarding the history of Israel at this period" when they try to interpret the passages relating to Antiochus.

R. D. Wilson points out: "They disagree among themselves and resort to many violent changes of the text in order to make it suit their conception of what it ought to be." 45/265

R. K. Harrison observes that if Daniel was the seer he was reputed to be, and there is no reason to doubt this, then his ability would be sufficient to describe the events in Daniel 11 and 12, which are as general as his earlier references to Antiochus Epiphanes. Harrison believes it also is apparent that Daniel was not as precise in the early chapters as the critics presume, evidenced by the possibility of confusion concering the little horns in Daniel 7:8 and 8:9. (The former cannot be Antiochus Epiphanes, while the latter is Antiochus.) A person contemporary with the events (*i.e.*, living in the Maccabean period) would not have allowed this ambiguousness to arise. 19/1130,1131

Pusey observes: "The argument against the book of Daniel involves broadly, that there are no true definite predictions in Holy Scripture, beyond the reach of human sagacity; else it could be no objection to the book of Daniel, that, if his, it has definite and minute predictions." 31/231

He adds: ". . . the argument, if honest, assumed the truth of prophecy generally. People, who so argue, act the believers in prophecy. For the alleged difference between the prophecies of Daniel and other prophecy could have no weight in disproving that they are Divine prophecy, unless it could be shewn, that they were so different in character from Divine prophecy, that it would be a contradiction to think that both came from the same Author." 31/265

Bleek, a critic, admits: "Yet it is not to be denied that, among the prophecies of the Hebrew prophets, there are several, even though few in comparison, which relate to single incidents of the future, and predict them. . . . *Yet we ought not, in this respect, to pass any overpositive judgment, since we are not in a condition to draw defined and sharp lines, how far and to what degree of definiteness the spirit of prophecy opens the future or not.* I do not then believe that, if the book of Daniel had all other marks of genuineness, the above-noticed character of the prophecies contained in it could be alleged as any certain proof of their later date." 31/231

3C. DIFFERENCES WITH EARLIER PROPHETICAL BOOKS

    1D. Arguments of the Radical Critics

        Besides the "minuteness of the predictions," Driver points out the following: "Its view of history is much more *comprehensive* than that of the earlier prophets.

        "It is remarkable also that Daniel — so unlike the prophets generally — should display no interest in the welfare, or prospects, of his contemporaries; that his hopes and Messianic visions should attach themselves, not (as is the case with Jer. Ez. Is. 40-66) to the approaching return of the exiles to the land of their fathers, but to the deliverance of his people in a remote future." 12/478,480

    2D. Answers

        One fallacy is basic in all of these arguments: the assumption that Daniel is a prophet in the same sense as the prophets of the Old Testament. As discussed in chapter 3, Daniel is not officially a prophet (see pp. 36,37) and, therefore, is not obligated to conform to the prophetical pattern.

        Also, a careful reading of Daniel 9 reveals that Daniel certainly was concerned about the welfare of his people, but not just their immediate, temporary welfare. He was concerned that the reason for the captivity was their continual disobedience to God's laws. He was aware of Israel's pattern of transgression and turning away from God, acts that were related to previous prophecies and dispersions of the Jewish people. Daniel entreated God to forgive the sins of His people and to remember His covenant with them.

        In answer, Daniel was shown God's purpose for choosing the Jewish nation and the culmination of that purpose in human history.

2B. Theological Arguments

The following arguments are based on the radical critics' view of the doctrines contained in the Book of Daniel. The critics contend that these doctrines are more advanced than the same doctrines of other books in the Old Testament, even in those books supposedly written after Daniel. They also claim that if Daniel is authentic, then its theology should have influenced the doctrines of the books written soon after Daniel was written.

1C. ARGUMENTS OF THE RADICAL CRITICS

S. R. Driver says: "The *theology* of the Book (in so far as it has a distinctive character) points to a later age than that of the exile." 12/477

He adds that "it is undeniable that the doctrines of the Messiah, of angels, of the resurrection, and of a judgment on the world, are taught with greater distinctness, and in a more developed form, than elsewhere in the OT., and with features approximating to (though not identical with) those met with in the earlier parts of the Book of Enoch, *c.* 100 B.C." 12/477

Driver concludes: "This atmosphere and tone are not those of any other writings belonging to the period of the exile: they are rather those of a stage intermediate between that of the early post-exilic and that of the early post-Biblical Jewish literature." 12/477

2C. ANSWERS

1D. The Critics' Fallacy

In essence, Driver and the critics have decided that various doctrines in the Bible evolved in a certain order, according to the Jews' expanding theological awareness.

But R. D. Wilson says that ". . . it is not fair to say without positive proof that the doctrines are late because they are in certain books or parts of books, and that the books or parts of books are late because they contain the doctrines. This, however, is exactly what the critics do. One of their principal reasons for putting Isa. xxiv,-xxvi, and Job late is the fact that the doctrine of the resurrection is taught in them. Joel is said to be late because of its prophecy on the judgment and the kingdom." 45/155

If a work makes no reference to the doctrines contained in Daniel, then the critics use this as evidence that it existed before Daniel was written. At least, this is what the critics claim concerning Haggai, Malachi and Chronicles. But if this argument is valid, then the third and fourth sections of Enoch; Jubilees; the Sibylline Oracles; the additions to Esther and Daniel; Tobit; Judith; I, III and IV Maccabees; Baruch; Wisdom; and the Psalms of Solomon also could have been written before Daniel. (Actually, they date around 150 B.C. and later.) 45/155

There are no marks of influence on a large portion of the Jewish literature that was written after 164 B.C., the alleged date of Daniel. 45/220

Of the four doctrines in Daniel which Driver uses as
evidence for Daniel's late date — the Messiah, angels, the
resurrection, the judgment — all are mentioned in Isaiah and
three are included in Zechariah. 45/215

Wilson comments: "While, on account of the reasons just
given, I think that we should not expect to find traces of the
ideas of Daniel in such works as Haggai, Esther, and Ezra, I
cannot see how there should be so few traces of these ideas in
the Psalms, if, as the critics assert, nearly all of them were
composed for the service of the second temple, and more
than fifty of them in Maccabean times. For example, is it not
remarkable that angels are so seldom mentioned in the
psalms, and that neither Gabriel, nor Michael, is named?
Why do so few of these numerous poems refer to the
Messiah, and why is the glorious and comforting doctrine of
the resurrection scarcely hinted at? The theories of *Zeitgeist*
and of traces of influence must not be used by the critics only
when they seem to support their assumptions. In the case of
the psalms, the theories are both dead against the critics."
45/221

2D. Daniel's Theology Not Advanced

Daniel's theology is as close to the theologies expressed in
the older books, such as Isaiah, Joel, Zechariah and certain
psalms, as it is to later writings, such as Enoch. 45/153,154

However, Daniel is one of the later books in the Old
Testament, even if written by Daniel, and would be expected
to have relatively advanced doctrine. 45/154

1E. The Messiah

In reference to the Messiah, several Old Testament works,
such as Isaiah, Zechariah and certain psalms, contain more
detail and are equally advanced. 45/154

Archer adds: "The concept of the Messiah appears as early
as Genesis 3:15 and 49:10; cf. also Numbers 24:17;
Deuteronomy 18:15; Isaiah 9:6,7; 11:1; Jeremiah 23:5,6;
33:11-17; Ezekiel 34:23-31; Micah 5:2." 3/395

In the Book of Enoch, the Messiah is symbolized as a white
bull with large horns (90:37). This is markedly different
from Daniel's view of the Messiah and cannot be the
product of an advancing theological concept, which the
critics claim both Daniel and Enoch exhibit. 50/363

2E. Angels

Two factors are noted: the naming of individual angels and
the recognition of hierarchical ranks among the angels.

John Raven asserts that Daniel is the only book in the Old Testament that names angels.

Wilson states: "If, however, the Jews derived the idea of naming angels from the Persians, how are we to account for the fact that of Old Testament writers Daniel alone gives names to angels? The critics assign about half of the literature of the Old Testament to Persian and Greek times; and of this literature, Daniel alone names angels, though it was written they tell us among the very latest of them all. Long after the Persian empire had ceased to exist, after the greatest of Alexander's successors had been crushed at Pydna and Magnesia, when the ashes of Corinth were lifting their grey bosom to the unheeding sun and the Roman legates were dictating peace to the rival monarchs of Syria and Egypt, this Persian idea, like a long lost seed, is supposed to have suddenly sprung up in Palestine, a thousand miles from the place of its birth and four hundred years after the time that Babylon fell before the arms of Cyrus. Believe it who can and will!" 45/193

Archer observes: "Concerning the ranks of angels, Genesis mentions cherubim, Joshua refers to a prince of the angels. Their function was said to be the delivery of messages to Abraham, Moses, Joshua, Gideon, and various prophets such as Isaiah, Zechariah, and Ezekiel. Thus as early as the Torah we find the angels revealing the will of God, furnishing protection for God's people, and destroying the forces of the enemy." 3/395

Concerning angels, Daniel is more advanced than other books in the Old Testament but closest in its concepts to Zechariah, another book of the sixth century B.C. 45/154

In Zechariah, the angels are distinguished by rank. The interpreting rule of angels in Zechariah (1:9,14,19; 2:3; 4:4-6,11-14; 5:5-11; 6:4-8) seems to be the same as Gabriel's in Daniel (8:16; 9:21). The angel of the Lord in Zechariah 3:1-3 (Jude 9) appears to be identical with Michael in Daniel (10:13,21; 12:1).

Young says: "In the doctrine of angels Daniel is similar to Enoch only in that he mentions Gabriel and Michael by name. Enoch says much more than does Daniel. Further, the doctrine of angels also appears throughout the Old Testament." 50/363

Daniel, therefore, is unique among Old Testament books because it names specific angels, but other than that, the book does not introduce novel angelic doctrine.

3E.   The Resurrection

In Isaiah 26:19 there is reference to the resurrection which
is as advanced as Daniel's doctrine of the resurrection, and
Isaiah without doubt is older than Daniel. 45/154

Archer expounds: "So far as the resurrection is concerned,
there is the famous affirmation of Job in Job 19:25,26
(although another interpretation of this passage is
possible); Isaiah's affirmation in 26:19 ('Thy dead shall
live; my dead bodies shall arise,' ASV); Ezekiel's vision of
the valley of dry bones, and possibly the resuscitation of
the dead by Elijah and Elisha. On the other hand, of the
large number of post-canonical works, only the Book of the
Twelve Patriarchs refers to a resurrection of both the
righteous and the wicked as is found in Daniel 12:2." 3/395

Young professes: "The doctrine of the resurrection is
found in several passages of the Old Testament, e.g., Isa.
26:19; 53:10; Ezek. 37; Job 19:25; I K. 17; II K. 4. Only in
12:2, does Daniel mention the resurrection, and this is not
similar to the mention of Enoch 25; 90:33." 50/365

Therefore, the doctrine of the resurrection in Daniel is
neither novel nor unique among Old Testament writings.

4E.   The Judgment

As for the judgment, Daniel certainly is developed no
more than Joel 3. 45/154

Isaiah, Zephaniah, Haggai, Zechariah, Malachi and many
of the psalms speak of the doctrine of the last judgment.
Often the judgment has reference to the world as well as
Israel.

Also, the Book of Enoch, like Daniel, states there will be a
judgment. 50/363

Again, Daniel's doctrine of the judgment, like his
doctrines of the Messiah, angels and the resurrection, is
not advanced for a sixth century B.C. writer. None of these
doctrines prove a late date for Daniel's composition.

3D. Influence Cannot Be Determined from Subsequent Writings

Although Haggai, Malachi, Chronicles, Ezra and Nehemiah
are silent on the doctrines of angels and the resurrection,
judgment and Messiah, can the critics know the thoughts of
the authors of these books on these doctrines?

The reason little trace of Daniel's influence is found on
post-165 B.C. literature is that these works deal with
different subjects than those of Daniel. 45/220,221

R. D. Wilson explains that "first, according to the opinion of both conservative and radical scholars, Haggai, Esther, Ezra, Nehemiah, Chronicles, and the first part of Zechariah, were composed after the return from captivity.

"Haggai, having been written about 520 B.C., can hardly be expected to show many traces of Daniel's influence. It has only thirty-eight verses, and the subject of his prophecy is the rebuilding of the temple. Mere silence, therefore, about the matters treated of in Daniel proves nothing as to what Haggai's views on these matters may have been.

"Zechariah, both in form and subject-matter, shows more likeness to the Book of Daniel than can be found in any other work of the Old Testament.

"Esther presents few traces of any earlier literature, and as the events narrated by its writer have no connection, historically or doctrinally, with the events and teachings of Daniel, it is hard to see that they are of such a character as that traces of Daniel should certainly be found in them." 45/218

"Malachi exhibits as many possible traces of Daniel as it does of Isaiah, Jeremiah, Ezekiel, and the other prophetic works. Chronicles purports to give the history of Israel down to the captivity alone. It would be an evident anachronism for its writer to have shown traces of the influence of a book written fifty years after the destruction of Jerusalem.

"Ezra and Nehemiah are largely personal memoirs, genealogies, and narratives concerning the building of the wall of Jerusalem and the reestablishment of the Law. They show slight traces of any of the prophets and none of most of them; why then should we expect to find large traces of Daniel in them? None but a critic's eye 'in a fine frenzy rolling' could have expected to trace the marks of Daniel's teachings on the great things of the kingdom amid the intricacies of the laws on intermarriage with heathen wives, amid the descriptions of the building of the wall, among the special injunctions for the observance of the Sabbath, or even in the account of the keeping of the feast of Tabernacles and of the renewal of the covenant. The prayer of Nehemiah, recorded in chapter nine of the book named after him, certainly has some resemblances to chapter nine of Daniel; but in the chapters themselves there is no evidence to show which of them copied from the other." 45/219

The Book of Zechariah strongly resembles Daniel in certain areas. The roles angels play in both books are so similar that a reasonable and strong deduction can be made that either Daniel influenced Zechariah, whose prophetic ministry ranged from 519 to 420 B.C., or Zechariah influenced Daniel. 3/394

R. D. Wilson succinctly sums up the critique concerning the necessity of finding Daniel's influence on later writings: "Is it necessary to suppose that every author of a book must have told all he knew on every subject, or that God must have given the same message to every writer of the same period, no matter what may have been the purpose of his writing, or the work he had to do?" 45/155,156

Although all the works alluded to (except Zechariah) are either immediately post-exilic or subsequent to 165 B.C., the date the critics claim Daniel was written, they contain nothing which can be traced specifically to Daniel; but since none of them (except Zechariah) discuss the same subjects as Daniel, this argument concerning influence on later works is futile.

3B. Supporting Historical Arguments

The following arguments are of an historical nature which the radical critics use to support, but not to prove, their late date theory of Daniel.

1C. ARGUMENTS OF THE RADICAL CRITICS

Driver lists the following historical features of Daniel that militate against early authorship.

1D. "The improbability that Daniel, a strict Jew, should have suffered himself to be initiated into the class of Chaldean 'wise men,' or should have been admitted by the wise men themselves (c. 1, cf. 2,13)." 12/469

2D. ". . . Nebuchadnezzar's 7 years' insanity ('lycanthropy'), with his edict respecting it." 12/469

3D. ". . . the absolute terms in which both he [Nebuchadnezzar] and Darius (4, 1-3. 34-37. 6, 25-27), while retaining, so far as appears, their idolatry, recognise the supremacy of the God of Daniel, and command homage to be done to Him." 12/469

2C. ANSWERS

Concerning the above arguments, Driver admits: "On these and some other similar considerations our knowledge is hardly such as to give us an objective criterion for estimating their cogency. The circumstances alleged will appear improbable or not improbable, according as the critic, upon *independent* grounds, has satisfied himself that the Book is the work of a later author, or written by Daniel himself. It would be hazardous to use the statements in question in *proof* of the late date of the Book; though, *if* its late date were established on other grounds, it would be not unnatural to regard some of them as involving an exaggeration of the actual fact." 12/469

1D. Daniel Avoided Occult Involvement

Although he was a wise man, Daniel did not participate in the occult. An example of Daniel's stand against indulging in practices contrary to Jewish customs is his refusal to eat the king's rich meat and wine (chapter 1). Surely if Daniel was careful not to disobey Jewish food customs, then he would be more careful not to disobey the plainly expressed directives in the Torah against participation in the occult. Although Daniel and his friends were instructed in the knowledge and language of the Chaldeans (1:4), there is no mention of instruction in the occult arts. In fact, Daniel and his friends had more wisdom and understanding than all the magicians and astrologers in the empire (1:20). Daniel and his friends are neither included among them nor accounted as fellow occultists.

Also, when the king ordered the magicians, astrologers, sorcerers and Chaldeans to tell his dream (2:2), Daniel and his friends were not among them. But when the king ordered all the wise men to be slain, Daniel and his friends were included (2:12,13). This seems to indicate that Daniel and his friends were considered wise men because of their knowledge and wisdom (1:17) and not because of their participation in the occult arts. It is clear (2:18) that Daniel and his friends considered themselves among the wise men.

In chapter 4, all the wise men again were ordered to appear before Nebuchadnezzar, but they could not interpret his dream. Then last, Daniel, the appointed head over all the wise men (2:48), went before the king (4:8).

Belshazzar also summoned all the wise men, including astrologers, Chaldeans and soothsayers, to interpret the omen (5:7). Again, Daniel was not among them, but he was known for his great wisdom (5:11,12).

It is clear, then, that although Daniel and his friends evidently were classed as wise men for a time, they did not engage in the occult methods of the other wise men. This is seen by the way Daniel approached each problem. Occult methods of acquiring knowledge are not God's methods, and a study of occult involvement reveals that the powers cannot be mixed. An individual receives power either from occult sources or from God, but never from both. An involvement with one source precludes available power from the other source. Both historical and biblical cases verify this.

Pusey says that Daniel did not necessarily have anything to do with magic, because the Chaldeans also studied "political and social legislation, philosophy, medicine, botony, natural history and the history of man. There was then a large field for Daniel to study or to regulate, without entering upon their superstitions or misbelief." 31/358

That Daniel was made *rab* over all the wise men does not mean he was one of them or practiced their particular arts. 44/387,388

Wilson declares: ". . . there is no evidence in the book of Daniel, nor anywhere else, to show that Daniel practiced the black art, nor the heathen methods of divination in any form, nor to show that he became a member of any of these orders. It is said simply that he was the superior of these in knowledge and wisdom and in power of interpretation of dreams and omens. The means he used were proper according to the precepts and examples of the Scriptures." 44/388

Young points out that Daniel's authority was political: "Daniel was made *'rab-signin'* (a political title) over all the wise men of Babylon — a very wise precaution. All the terms used of Daniel and the three other youths in Daniel 1:4,17, and 20 are of the most innocent kind, and relate in no way to either priesthood or magic." 51/273

It should be noted that in both the sixth and second centuries B.C., a wise man was held in high esteem. 44/367,368

If Moses was taught in all the wisdom of Egypt and if Paul attended a heathen university in Tarsus, surely it was not improper for Daniel to be instructed in the learning of the Chaldeans. 44/372

The Book of Daniel says only that Daniel was given political authority over the wise men, not that he became a member of some order. But Young points out: "If the book of Daniel really teaches that Daniel became a heathen priest, as apparently some critics think it does, would not such teaching be one of the strongest arguments against a post-exilic origin for the book? In the third century B.C. when Jewish nationalism was being emphasized, how can we conceive of a 'legendary' Jewish hero becoming a heathen priest? And if this narrative is from Maccabean times, how can such a representation possibly be accounted for?" 50/357,358

The critics have failed to consider that, if it was wrong for a sixth century Jew to be a wise man, then why would a second century Jew call his hero a wise man?

2D. Nebuchadnezzar's Madness

Early sources testify of the plausibility for Nebuchadnezzar's insanity.

Young remarks: "Berossus also (*Contra Apionem* 1:20) remarks that after a reign of 43 years, Nebuchadnezzar, after beginning the construction of a certain wall, fell sick and died. The Greek text conveys the idea that the king was *suddenly invaded by sickness*. Now sickness before death is so common that there would be no point in mentioning it, were it not of an unusual kind. Hence, here also, we probably have a garbled reflection upon the tragedy which overcame the king. But it should be remembered that, even if history (apart from the Bible) was silent upon the subject of the king's madness, that in itself is not a sufficient reason for denying the historicity of the account in Daniel." 50/358

Young also says: "In his *Praeparatio Evangelica* (9:41) Eusebius gives a quotation from Abydenus, which describes the last days of Nebuchadnezzar. It relates that, 'being possessed by some god or other,' the king went up to his palace and announced the coming of a Persian mule (i.e., Cyrus), who would bring the people into slavery. Then says Abydenus, 'He, when he had uttered this prediction, immediately disappeared.' These last words seem to have reference to the king's madness, which is covered up under the form of a prediction. Thus, in Abydenus' time there was in existence a tradition about something peculiar and extraordinary having occurred toward the close of Nebuchadnezzar's life. It should be noted that the king is thought to have been seized by some divinity; he was on his palace, as Daniel also states; and this event occurred after the king's conquest and shortly before his death." 50/358

Another important reference is found in the Dead Sea Scrolls, the Prayer of Nabonidus from Cave IV. It reads as follows: "The words of the prayer made by Nabonidus, king of (Assyria) and of Babylon, (the great) king, (when he was smitten) with a malignant disease, by the decree of the (Most High God, in the town of) Teima. 'I was smitten (with a malignant disease) for a period of seven years, and became unlike (men. But when I had confessed my sins) and faults, God vouchsafed me a magician. He was a Jew from among (those exiled in Babylon). He gave his explanation, and wrote an order that honour and (great glory) should be given to the Name of the (Most High God. And thus he wrote: While) you were smitten with a (malignant) disease (in the town of) Teima (by decree of the Most High God), you prayed for seven years (to gods) of silver and gold, (of bronze, iron), wood, stone and clay. . . .' " 79/36,37

Although this refers to Nabonidus rather than Nebuchadnezzar, it shows the plausibility of this condition as well as its association with a Babylonian king.

Even the relatively recent liberal commentary by Porteous acknowledges some relationship between the Nabodinus legend and the account in Daniel of Nebuchadnezzar. He states: "Still more remarkable is the parallel in the Prayer of Nabonidus found at Qumran (Burrows, *More Light on the Dead Sea Scrolls*, p. 400) which tells how the king was laid low at Teima by an inflammation of some kind and during his seven years' illness had to be segregated from human society. We are told that upon his repentance, a Jewish seer urged him to give glory to the name of the Most High God, whereas at the beginning of his illness he had prayed to idols." 77/72

3D.   Nebuchadnezzar's Homage to God of Israel

Boutflower explains how Nebuchadnezzar could retain his idolatry and at the same time recognize the supremacy of Jehovah: "When Merodach became the Enlil [the chief god], the other gods, as we have seen, bestowed on him their names and attributes. This fable of Babylonian mythology tended in the direction of monotheism, and paved the way for the identification of the other deities with Merodach, and for regarding them as so many manifestations of Merodach. This appears most clearly in a tablet known as the Monotheistic Tablet, from which the following is an extract: —

'Ninib is Merodach of the garden (?).
Nergal is Merodach of war.
Zagaga is Merodach of battle.
Enlil is Merodach of lordship and dominion.
Nebo is Merodach of trading.
Sin is Merodach the illuminator of the night.
Shamash is Merodach of righteousness.
Rimmon is Merodach of rain.'

"How easy, then, would it be for the great king of Babylon, who was so devoted to his god, to add to this list and say — 'Jehovah is Merodach the revealer of secrets,' thus acknowledging the God of Israel as one out of many manifestations of the Most High God!" 4/98,99

Another possible explanation is that Nebuchadnezzar designated Jehovah as the Enlil, or chief god. Boutflower says: "Our study, then, of Inscription 15 has led us to the conclusion that not only was there a tendency towards monotheism in the Babylonian religion, but that Nebuchadnezzar himself became increasingly monotheistic in his later years, a circumstance which might well be expected in view of the great miracles recorded in the Book of Daniel." 4/98

Boutflower affirms the possibility of Nebuchadnezzar paying homage to God: "If, then, Nabopolassar could include Shamash in the Enlilship along with Merodach, and if Nabonidus could bestow the title at one time on Merodach at another on Sin, it can be no matter of surprise to us to find Nebuchadnezzar, under the influence of the mighty miracles wrought before his eyes, bestowing on the God of the Jews the titles 'the Most High' and the 'Most High God.' " 4/101

4B. Supporting Linguistic Argument

1C. ARGUMENT OF THE RADICAL CRITICS

The radical critics often maintain that the use of the two languages (Hebrew and Aramaic) indicates the Book of Daniel was written by more than one author.

2C. ANSWERS

The following evidence supports the unity of Daniel:

1. The first part of the book introduces the second, and the second part is not understandable without the first part.

2. The various themes of the book are interwoven and interdependent.

3. All of the historical narratives have the same purpose — to reveal how God is glorified through pagan nations.

4. Daniel appears as the same person throughout the book.

Eisfeldt, a liberal critic, comments: ". . . it must be said at the outset that this divergence in the assessment of the formation of the Book of Daniel may be explained largely on the grounds that both Rowley and Ginsberg occasionally derive *precise* verdicts from very *imprecise* evidence. They are trying to discover more than can here be discovered, and so go against a basic principle which they both recognize as binding. . . ." 13/519

Harrison remarks: "The foregoing selection will be sufficient to indicate the great divergence of opinion regarding the questions of integrity and authorship, and, by implication, the date of the book or its supposed parts. This very situation is unfortunately self-defeating, for as Rowley has pointed out, if there is so little consensus of opinion as to which were the earlier parts, it is difficult to have much confidence in the method whereby these varying results were reached.

"Arguments for diversity of authorship on the ground that the book contains two languages can no longer be sustained in the light of current information regarding the literary patternism of the ancient Near East. As has already been mentioned in connection with Job, the device of enclosing the main body of a composition within the linguistic form of a contrasting style so as to heighten the effect of the work was commonly employed in the construction of single, integrated writings in the corpus of Mesopotamian literature. On the basis of this evidence, therefore, Daniel ought to be understood to form a unified and consciously formulated literary integer, involving Aramaic and Hebrew components." 19/1109,1110

Keil comments: "With this the change in the language of the book agrees. The first part (ch. ii.-vii.), treating of the world-power and its development, is written in Chaldee, which is the language of the world-power; the second part (ch. viii.-xii.), treating of the kingdom of God and its development, as also the first chapter, which shows how Daniel the Israelite was called to be a prophet by God, is written in the Hebrew, which is the language of the people of God. This circumstance denotes that in the first part the fortunes of the world-power, and that in the second part the development of the kingdom of God, is the subject treated of (cf. Auber. p. 39, Klief. p. 44).

"From these things we arrive at the certainty that the book of Daniel forms an organic whole, as is now indeed generally acknowledged, and that it was composed by a prophet according to a plan resting on higher illumination." 23/19

Young summarizes: "There does not appear to be any truly satisfactory explanation of the two languages. The explanation which seems to be freest from difficulty is that the use of two languages was deliberate and intentional upon the part of the author. Aramaic was used for those parts which dealt primarily with the world nations, and Hebrew for those which treated principally the future of the kingdom of God. This view is surely not free from difficulty, but on the whole it appears to be the most satisfactory." 50/367

Although Daniel was a Hebrew, Aramaic was the dominant language of the time and place in which he lived. Therefore, it is not unusual that he should write using both languages. 3/390,391

BIBLIOGRAPHY

1. Allis, Oswald T. *The Old Testament, Its Claims and Its Critics.* Nutley, N.J.: The Presbyterian and Reformed Publishing Co., 1972.

2. Anderson, Sir Robert. *The Coming Prince.* London: Pickering and Inglis Ltd., n.d.

3. Archer, Gleason L. *A Survey of Old Testament Introduction.* Chicago: Moody Press, 1973.

4. Boutflower, Charles. *In and Around the Book of Daniel.* London: Society for Promoting Christian Knowledge, 1923.

5. Bulman, James M. "The Identification of Darius the Mede." *The Westminster Theological Journal.* Vol. 35, No. 3, Spring 1973, pp. 247-267.

6. Burrows, Millar. *What Mean These Stones?* New York: Meridian Books, 1957.

7. Cartledge, S. A. *A Conservative Introduction to the Old Testament.* Grand Rapids: Zondervan Publishing House, 1943.

8. Driver, S. R. "Daniel." *Cambridge Bible.* Cambridge, at the University Press, 1901.

9. Clinton, Stephen M. "S. R. Driver and the Date of Daniel." *The Journal of Church and Society.* Vol. V, No. 2, Fall 1969, pp. 30-41.

10. Cobern, C. M. "Alexander the Great." *The International Standard Bible Encyclopedia.* Grand Rapids: Wm. B. Eerdmans Publishing Co., 1939.

11. Dougherty, Raymond P. *Nabonidus and Belshazzar.* New Haven: Yale University Press, 1929.

12. Driver, S. R. *An Introduction to the Literature of the Old Testament.* Edinburgh: T & T Clark, 1898.

13. Eisfeldt, Otto. "Daniel." *The Old Testament — An Introduction.* Translated by Peter R. Alkroyd. New York: Harper and Row, 1965.

14. Free, J. P. *Archaeology and Bible History.* Wheaton, Illinois: Scripture Press Publications, 1969.

15. Frost, S. B. "Daniel." *The Interpreter's Dictionary of the Bible.* Edited by George A. Buttrick. New York: Abingdon Press, 1962.

16. Gruenthauer, Michael J. "The Last King of Babylon." *Catholic Biblical Quarterly.* Vol. XI, 1949, pp. 406-427.

17. Harris, R. L. "Factors Promoting the Formation of the Old Testament Canon." *Bulletin of the Evangelical Theological Society.* Vol. 9, Fall 1966, pp. 163-171.

18. Harris, R. L. "Was the Law and the Prophets Two-thirds of the Old Testament Canon?" *Bulletin of the Evangelical Theological Society.* Vol. 10, Winter 1967, pp. 21-27.

19. Harrison, R. K. *Introduction to the Old Testament.* Grand Rapids: Wm. B. Eerdmans Publishing Co., 1969.

20. Hsieh, Andrew. *Some Problems in the Aramaic Portions of the Book of Daniel.* A thesis presented to the faculty of the department of Semitics and Old Testament at Talbot Theological Seminary, June 1961.

21. Jenkins, Erwin. *The Authorship of Daniel.* A thesis presented to the faculty of the department of Old Testament at Talbot Theological Seminary, June 1955.

22. Josephus, Flavius. *Josephus' Complete Works.* Translated by William Whiston. Grand Rapids: Kregel Publications, 1960.

23. Keil, C. F. *Biblical Commentary on the Book of Daniel.* Translated by M. G. Easton. Grand Rapids: Wm. B. Eerdmans Publishing Co., n.d.

24. Kraeling, E. G. *The Brooklyn Museum Aramaic Papyri.* New Haven: Yale University Press, 1953.

25. Langdon, S. H. *Historical Inscriptions, Containing Principally the Chronological Prism.* London: Oxford University Press, 1923.

26. Lange, John P. *Daniel Lange's Commentary on the Holy Scripture.* Grand Rapids: Zondervan Publishing House, 1876.

27. Pfeiffer, R. H. *Introduction to the Old Testament.* rev. ed. New York: Harper, 1948.

28. Pierson, A. T. *Many Infallible Proofs.* New York: Fleming H. Revell Co., 1886.

29. Price, I. M. *The Monuments and the Old Testament.* Philadelphia: Judson Press, 1925.

30. Pritchard, J. B. (ed.) *Ancient Near Eastern Texts Relating to the Old Testament.* 2nd ed. Princeton: Princeton Univ. Press, 1955.

31. Pusey, E. B. *Daniel the Prophet.* New York: Funk and Wagnalls, 1885.

32. Raven, John H. *Old Testament Introduction.* London: Fleming H. Revell Co., 1910.

33. Rhodes, A. B. "The Book of Daniel." *Interpretation.* Vol. VI, 1952, pp. 436-450.

34. Rowley, H. H. *The Servant of the Lord and Other Essays on the Old Testament.* London: Lutterworth Press, 1952.

35. Sayce, A. H. *The Higher Criticism and the Verdict of the Monuments.* London: Society for Promoting Christian Knowledge, 1895.

36. Scott, R. B. Y. (sup) "Daniel, Book of." *Twentieth Century Encyclopedia of Religious Knowledge.* Editor-in-chief, Lefferts A. Loetscher. Grand Rapids: Baker Book House, 1955.

37. Smith, Sidney. *Babylonian Historical Texts Relating to the Captivity and Downfall of Babylon.* London: Methuen and Co., Ltd., 1924.

38. Tacitus. *The Histories.* Translated by Clifford H. Moore. (From the Loeb Classical Library, edited by T. E. Page) Cambridge: Harvard University Press, 1956.

39. Thiele, E. R. *The Mysterious Numbers of the Hebrew Kings.* Chicago: University of Chicago Press, 1951.

40. Thomson, J. E. H. "Daniel: An Exposition." *The Pulpit Commentary*. Edited by Spence and Exell. New York: Funk and Wagnalls, 1896.

41. Unger, Merril F. *Archaeology and the Old Testament*. Grand Rapids: Zondervan Publishing House, 1972.

42. Whitcomb, John C. *Darius the Mede*. Philadelphia: Presbyterian and Reformed Publishing Co., 1963.

43. Wilson, Joseph D. *Did Daniel Write Daniel?* New York: Charles C. Cook, n.d.

44. Wilson, R. D. *Studies in the Book of Daniel, A Discussion of the Historical Questions*. New York: The Knickerbocker Press, 1917.

45. Wilson, R. D. *Studies in the Book of Daniel, Second Series*. New York: Fleming H. Revell Co., 1938.

46. Wiseman, D. J. *Chronicles of Chaldean Kings*. London: Trustees of the British Museum, 1961.

47. Wiseman, Donald J., and others. *Notes on Some Problems in the Book of Daniel*. London: The Tyndale Press, 1970.

48. Yaron, R. *Introduction to the Law of the Aramaic Papyri*. Oxford, at the Clarendon Press (Oxford University Press), 1961.

49. Young, Edward J. "The Prophecy of Daniel." *Christianity Today*. Vol. 1, February 4, 1957, pp. 19 ff.

50. Young, Edward J. *An Introduction to the Old Testament*. Grand Rapids: Wm. B. Eerdmans Publishing Co., 1956.

51. Young, E. J. *The Prophecy of Daniel*. Grand Rapids: Wm. B. Eerdmans Publishing Co., 1949.

52. Curtis, E. L. "Daniel." *Hastings Dictionary of the Bible*. New York: Charles Scribner's Sons, 1898.

53. Newell, William R. *Old Testament Studies*. Toronto: L. S. Haynes Press, 1908.

54. Gaebelein, A. C. *The Prophet Daniel*. New York: Our Hope Press, 1911.

55. Cornill, C. H. *Introduction to the Canonical Books of the Old Testament*. Translated by G. H. Box. New York: G. P. Putman's Sons, 1907.

56. Miller, H. S. *General Biblical Introduction*. Houghton, New York: Word Bearer Press, 1947.

57. Baxter, J. Sidlow. *Explore the Book*. Grand Rapids: Zondervan Publishing House, 1960.

58. Burrows, Millar. *The Dead Sea Scrolls*. New York: Viking Press, 1955.

59. Finegan, Jack. *Handbook of Biblical Chronology*. Princeton: Princeton University Press, 1964.

60. Albright, W. F. "The Date and Personality of the Chronicler." *Journal of Biblical Literature*. Vol. 40, 1921, pp. 104-124.

61. Driver, G. R. "The Aramaic of the Book of Daniel" and "The Aramaic Language." *Journal of Biblical Literature*. Vol. 45, 1926, pp. 110 ff., 323 ff.

62. Pinches, T. G. "Fresh Light on the Book of Daniel." *The Expository Times*. Vol. 26, April 1915, pp. 297-299.

63. Tadmor, M. "Chronology of the Last Kings of Judah." *Journal of Near Eastern Studies*. Vol. 15, October 1956, pp. 226-230.

64. "Fragments of the Book of Daniel Found." *The Archaeological News and Views*. Vol. 12, No. 2, May 1949, p. 33.

65. Whitcomb, J. C. *Darius the Mede*. Grand Rapids: Wm. B. Eerdmans Publishing Co., 1959.

66. Keller, Werner. *The Bible as History*. Translated by William Neil. New York: Wm. Morrow and Co., 1956.

67. Rawlinson, George. *Egypt and Babylonia*. New York: Alden Publishers, 1885.

68. Rowley, H. H. *Darius the Mede and the Four World Empires in the Book of Daniel*. Cardiff: University Wales Press Board, 1935.

69. Martin, W. J. "Daniel, Book of." *The New Bible Dictionary*. Grand Rapids: Wm. B. Eerdmans Publishing Co., 1962.

70. Barton, G. A. *Archaeology and the Bible*. 7th ed. Philadelphia: American Sunday School Union, 1937.

71. McDowell, Josh. *Evidence That Demands a Verdict*. San Bernardino: Campus Crusade for Christ International, 1972.

72. Orr, James, editor. *International Standard Bible Encyclopedia*. 5 volumes. Grand Rapids: Wm. B. Eerdmans Publishing Co., 1946.

73. Hoehner, H. W. *Chronological Aspects of the Life of Christ*. Grand Rapids: Zondervan Publishing House, 1977.

74. Waltke, B. K. "The Date of the Book of Daniel." *Bibliotheca Sacra*. October-December 1976, Vol. 133:532, pp. 319-329.

75. Anderson, R. *Daniel in the Critics' Den*. London: James Nisbet & Co., Ltd., 1902.

76. Payne, J. Barton, editor. *New Perspectives on the Old Testament*. Waco, Texas: Word Publishers, 1970.

77. Porteous, Norman W. *Daniel*. Philadelphia: The Westminster Press, 1965.

78. Allis, O. T. *Unity of Isaiah*. Philadelphia: Presbyterian Reformed Publishing Co., 1950.

79. Milik, J. T. *Ten Years of Discovery in the Wilderness of Judaea*. Naperville, Illinois: Alec R. Allen Son, Inc., 1959.

80. Cross, Frank Moore, Jr. *The Ancient Library of Qumran and Modern Biblical Studies*. Garden City, N.Y.: Archer Books, Doubleday Co., 1961.

81. Yamauchi, Edwin. *Greece and Babylon*. Grand Rapids: Baker Book House, 1967.

82. Burrows, Millar. *More Light on the Dead Sea Scrolls*. New York: Viking Press, 1958.

83. Myers, Jacob M. "I Chronicles." *Anchor Bible.* New York: Doubleday Co., 1965.
84. Dupont-Sommer, A. *Dead Sea Scrolls; A Preliminary Study.* Translated by E. Margaret Rowley. Oxford: Basil Blackwell, 1952.
85. Brownlee, W. H. *The Meaning of the Dead Sea Scrolls.* New York: Oxford University Press, 1964.
86. Rowley, H. H. *The Zadokite Fragments and the Dead Sea Scrolls.* Oxford: Basil Blackwell, 1956.
87. Archer, Gleason. "The Aramaic of the 'Genesis Apocryphon' Compared with the Aramaic of Daniel." *New Perspectives on the Old Testament.* Edited by J. Barton Payne. Waco, Texas: Word Publishers, 1970.
88. Anderson, Bernard W. *Understanding the Old Testament.* Englewood Cliffs, New Jersey: Prentiss-Hall, Inc., 1966.

Biographical Sketches of Authors

Albright, W. F., Ph.D., Litt.D., was the W. W. Spence Professor of Semitic Languages and Chairman, Oriental Seminary at Johns Hopkins University. He taught at Johns Hopkins from 1929 to 1958. He was president of the International Organization of Old Testament Scholars, director of the American School of Oriental Research in Jerusalem, and led a number of archaeological expeditions in the Middle East. He is the author of more than 800 publications on archaeological, biblical and Oriental subjects. In 1933 he described his position as "neither conservative nor radical in the usual sense of the terms" (*Bulletin of the American Schools of Oriental Research,* No. 51, September 1933, pp. 5,6).

Allis, Oswald T., is a graduate of the University of Pennsylvania (B.A.), Princeton Theological Seminary (B.D.) and the University of Berlin (Ph.D.). He holds an honorary doctor of divinity degree from Hampden Sydney College. He taught in the department of Semitic philology at Princeton Theological Seminary and served as professor in the Old Testament department of Westminster Theological Seminary.

Anderson, Sir Robert (1841-1918), was a British barrister and writer. Born in Dublin, Ireland, he was educated at Trinity College, Dublin, and entered the legal profession in 1863. In addition to law and criminal investigation, he devoted much time to theological study. He is the author of many books, including *Daniel in the Critics' Den.*

Archer, Gleason L., Jr., is chairman of the division of Old Testament at Trinity Evangelical Divinity School, Deerfield, Ill. He holds a B.A., M.A. and Ph.D. from Harvard; an LL.B. from Suffolk University Law School, Boston; and a B.D. from Princeton Seminary. He is the author of *A Survey of Old Testament Introduction.*

Burrows, Millar, earned his B.A. from Cornell, B.D. from Union Theological Seminary, Ph.D. from Yale and honorary D.D. from Yale. He was a professor of Bible at Tusculum College and a professor of Bible and religion at Brown University. For 24 years a professor of biblical theology at Yale Divinity School, he has been professor emeritus there since 1958. He has authored four books, including *The Dead Sea Scrolls.*

Driver, Sir Godfrey Rolles, received honorary doctor of divinity degrees from Aberdeen and Manchester and honorary doctor of letters degrees from Durham, Oxford and Cambridge. The son of S. R. Driver, he was vice president of Magdalen College, Hebrew lecturer at St. John's College and professor of Semitic philology at Oxford. He was joint director of the New English Bible translation, joint editor of the *Journal of Theological Studies* and is the author of books and articles on Semitic languages and the Old Testament.

Driver, Samuel Rolles (1846-1914), was the first to attempt an English translation of principles of Hebrew syntax in philosophical and scientific terms in his *Use of the Tenses in Hebrew*. His reputation as a Hebraist gained him a seat on the Old Testament revision committee (1875-1884). He was 31 years as Regius Professor of Hebrew and as a canon of Christ Church, Oxford.

Finegan, Jack, holds an A.B., M.A., B.D. and LL.D. from Drake University; a B.D. and M.Th. from Colgate-Rochester Divinity School; and a Litt.D. from Chapman College. He was professor of religious education at Iowa State College, professor of New Testament at Pacific School of Religion, Berkeley, and director of the Palestine Institute of Archaeology.

Free, Joseph P., holds a B.A., M.A. and Ph.D. from Princeton. He served as a professor of Bible and archaeology at Wheaton College and as chairman of the department of anthropology and archaeology at the same school. Since 1966 he has been a professor of history and archaeology at Bemidji State College.

Harris, R. Laird, is associate dean of the faculty and professor of Old Testament at Covenant Theological Seminary, St. Louis, Missouri. He has also been a visiting lecturer at Trinity Evangelical Divinity School in Deerfield, Illinois. He holds a Ph.D. from Dropsie College, Philadelphia.

Harrison, R. K., is professor of Old Testament at Wycliffe College, University of Toronto. Formerly he was head of the department of Hebrew at the University of Western Ontario and Hellmuth Professor of Old Testament at Huron College. He holds B.D., M.Th. and Ph.D. degrees from the University of London.

Hoehner, Harold Walter, is director of doctoral studies at Dallas Theological Seminary. He holds a B.A. from Barrington College, a Th.M. and Th.D. from Dallas Theological Seminary and a Ph.D. from Cambridge. He was an associate professor of New Testament literature and exegesis at Dallas Theological Seminary and an associate editor of *Bibliotheca Sacra*.

Jenkins, Erwin, is pastor of Grace Baptist Church, Santa Rosa, Calif. He holds a B.A. from Biola College and a B.D. from Talbot Theological Seminary.

Payne, John Barton, is professor of Old Testament at Trinity Seminary, Chicago. He has degrees of B.A. and M.A. from the University of California, B.D. from San Francisco Theological Seminary, and Th.M. and Th.D. from Princeton Theological Seminary.

Pfeiffer, Robert H., was a professor at Harvard University and Boston University. His writings include *Introduction to the Old Testament* (1941) and *History of New Testament Times,* with an introduction to the apocrypha (1949).

Raven, John Howard, was a long-standing professor of Old Testament language and exegesis at the theological seminary of the Reformed Church in America, New Brunswick, New Jersey.

Rowley, H. H., was professor of Hebrew language and literature at Manchester University, England.

Unger, Merrill F., holds a B.A. and Ph.D. from Johns Hopkins University and a Th.M. and Th.D. from Dallas Theological Seminary. For one year he was associate professor of Greek at Gordon College-Divinity School, but since 1948 has been professor of Old Testament and Semitics and emeritus professor at Dallas Theological Seminary. *Unger's Bible Dictionary* and *Unger's Bible Handbook* are two of the several major works he has authored.

Waltke, Bruce K., was professor of Semitics and Old Testament at Dallas Theological Seminary. He holds a B.A. from Houghton College, a Th.M. and Th.D. from Dallas Theological Seminary and a Ph.D. from Harvard University. He is currently on the faculty of Regents College, Vancouver, British Columbia.

Whitcomb, John Clement, Jr., is professor of theology and Old Testament and director of postgraduate studies at Grace Theological Seminary. He graduated *cum laude* (A.B.) from Princeton and holds a B.D., Th.M. and Th.D. from Grace Theological Seminary. He is the author of several books, including *Darius the Mede.*

Wilson, Robert Dick, attended Princeton University, Western Theological Seminary and the University of Berlin. He was professor of Old Testament at Western Theological Seminary, professor of Semitic philology and Old Testament introduction at Princeton Theological Seminary and cofounder of Westminster Theological Seminary. His writings include *Studies in the Book of Daniel, Is the Higher Criticism Scholarly?* and *Scientific Investigation of the Old Testament.*

Wiseman, Donald J., has served since 1948 as Assistant Keeper of the
Department of Egyptian and Assyrian (now Western Asiatic)
Antiquities of the British Museum. Educated at King's College,
London, and Wadham College, Oxford, he has excavated at
Nimrud, Iraq, and Harran, South Turkey, and has served on
archaeology survey teams in other Near Eastern countries. He is
professor of assyriology at London University.

Yamauchi, Edwin M., is associate professor of history at Miami
University, Oxford, Ohio. He has a Ph.D. in Mediterranean
studies from Brandeis University. His latest book is *The Stones and
the Scripture*.

Yaron, Reuven, studied at Hebrew University, Jerusalem, and the
University of Aberdeen, and he earned a Ph.D. at Oxford. Since
1968 he has been professor of Roman and ancient Near East law at
Hebrew University.

Young, Edward, holds a Ph.D. degree from Dropsie College,
Philadelphia, with additional study at the Lewman School of
Missions in Jerusalem, *Centro de Estudios Historicos* in Madrid,
and the University of Leipzig. His writings include *Introduction to
the Old Testament* and *Studies in Isaiah*. He was professor of Old
Testament at Westminster Seminary.

AUTHOR INDEX

SUBJECT INDEX

E

Ecclesiastes, 26
Ecclesiasticus, 40-45, 105
Elephantine Papyri, 87-89, 102
Esther, 11-12, 119
Exegetical Arguments, 109-114
Ezekiel, 27, 104-105
Ezra, 83-88, 93-94, 119

F

Four Empires, 22-25

G

Genesis Apocryphon, 87
Greek Words, 95-102
    Daniel, absence from, 97-98
Greek Influence, 98-101
Gubaru, 75-77

H

Haggai, 119
Hebrew, 102-107, 125-126
    Chronicles, of, 104
    Daniel, of, 104-105
    Development, 103
    Ecclesiasticus, of, 105
    Ezekiel, of, 104, 105
    Greek words, absence of, 104
    Nehemiah, of, 105
    Specific contested words,
        105-107

J

Jehoiachin, 47-49, 51
Jehoiakim, 45-49, 51-52, 54
Jeremiah, 45, 51-54, 78, 79
Jesus Christ, 2-3
    Crucifixion, 19
    Daniel, use of, 2-3, 29-31
    Triumphal entry, 19-20
Jewish Canon
    Daniel, position of, 33-34,
        37-38
    Daniel's acceptance, 38-40
    Divisions, 33
    Formation, 35-36
Joseph, 37, 41, 44-45
Josiah, 51